Praise for *God's To-Do List*

"A rich tapestry of stories and sayings that encourage us all to make ourselves and our world better through concrete actions that any of us could—and should—do."
—Rabbi Elliot N. Dorff, rector and distinguished professor of philosophy, University of Judaism; author, *The Way Into* Tikkun Olam *(Repairing the World)*

"Warm and welcoming … teaches us how to let God into our lives. Will touch your soul and possibly change your life."
—Sandy Eisenberg Sasso, author, *God's Paintbrush* and *In God's Name*

"For anyone who wants to help people grow in their relationship with God. Filled with the rich prayers and deep wisdom of the Jewish tradition that can help people of all faiths, all ages, reflect on their relationship with God."
—Fr. Steven E. Boes, executive director, Girls and Boys Town

"Filled with one wonderful suggestion after another for those who want to do good, but find that what we really need are concrete suggestions on what to do. Specific and inspiring, a much needed book."
—Rabbi Joseph Telushkin, author, *Jewish Literacy* and *A Code of Jewish Ethics*

"Wise, accessible and impassioned … suggests simple ways to make life meaningful, improve the world, and experience God's holiness. Invites the reader to see the world afresh and take part daily in Jewish living."
—Rabbi David Teutsch, PhD, author, *Spiritual Community*

"Sets out clearly what it means to live with purpose. I'm copying this wisdom into my daily calendar to be sure I get to all the items on God's To-Do List. You should too!"
—Rabbi Edward Feinstein, author,
Tough Questions Jews Ask: A Young Adult's Guide to Building a Jewish Life

"Combines Jewish text, real-life stories, and practical suggestions to the ultimate end that we should consider our place in life and mold that life with an element of holiness."
—Danny Siegel, author, *Giving Your Money Away;* poet and lecturer

"A powerful, accessible, practical guide to repairing the world—will inspire all who read it."
—Rabbi David Saperstein, director, Religious Action Center of Reform Judaism

Other Jewish Lights books by Dr. Ron Wolfson

Hanukkah, 2nd Edition: The Family Guide to Spiritual Celebration

Passover, 2nd Edition: The Family Guide to Spiritual Celebration

Shabbat, 2nd Edition: The Family Guide to Preparing for and Celebrating the Sabbath

The Spirituality of Welcoming: How to Transform Your Congregation into a Sacred Community

A Time to Mourn, a Time to Comfort, 2nd Edition: A Guide to Jewish Bereavement

What You Will See Inside a Synagogue (with Rabbi Lawrence A. Hoffman)

God's To-Do List

103 Ways to Be an Angel and Do God's Work on Earth

Dr. Ron Wolfson

For People of All Faiths, All Backgrounds

JEWISH LIGHTS Publishing

Woodstock, Vermont

God's To-Do List:
103 Ways to Be an Angel and Do God's Work on Earth

2007 Third Printing
2007 Second Printing
2007 First Printing
© 2007 by Ron Wolfson

For information regarding permission to reprint material from this book, please mail or fax your request in writing to Jewish Lights Publishing, Permissions Department, at the address / fax number listed below, or e-mail your request to permissions@jewishlights.com.

Malvina Reynolds lyrics reprinted by permission of Universal-Northern Music Publishing Group.

Library of Congress Cataloging-in-Publication Data
Wolfson, Ron.
God's to-do list : 103 ways to be an angel and do God's work on earth / Ron Wolfson.
p. cm.
Includes bibliographical references.
ISBN-13: 978-1-58023-301-9 (quality pbk.)
ISBN-10: 1-58023-301-5 (quality pbk.)
1. Jewish way of life. 2. Jewish ethics. I. Title.
BM723.W65 2006
296.7—dc22

2006027733

10 9 8 7 6 5 4 3

Cover design: Sara Dismukes

Manufactured in the United States of America

For People of All Faiths, All Backgrounds
Published by Jewish Lights Publishing
A Division of LongHill Partners, Inc.
Sunset Farm Offices, Route 4, P.O. Box 237
Woodstock, VT 05091
Tel: (802) 457-4000   Fax: (802) 457-4004
www.jewishlights.com

Contents

For Susie
my angel

Acknowledgments

I am blessed with many family members, friends, and colleagues who supported the writing of this book. They have been unfailingly generous with their comments, suggestions and encouragement. My thanks to Bernice and Alan Wolfson, Bob and Sibby Wolfson, Doug and Sara Wolfson, Nancy and Don Greenberg, Rabbi Bernard and Harriet Lipnick, Ann and Nate Levine, Larry Hoffman, Craig Taubman, Jan Antczak, Rabbi Ed Feinstein, Fr. Richard Vosko, Pastor Rick Warren, and Carolyn Starman Hessel, who read early drafts and offered guidance. Stuart Matlins, publisher and editor in chief of Jewish Lights, believed in the idea from the moment I presented it to him. He and his superb team—Lauren Seidman, Emily Wichland, Sara Dismukes, Tim Holtz, Kristi Menter, and Jenny Buono—gave the project special attention and care. I am honored that many significant leaders representing many faith traditions have endorsed the book.

To those real life angels whose stories are told in this volume, my heartfelt appreciation. Havi and Michael, my two very adult children, have always given me permission to tell stories about them through the years, knowing that Dad, at heart, is a teacher—and teachers need stories that illustrate life lessons. Everyone needs a "guardian angel" and mine is Susie Kukawka Wolfson. You are my wings, my prayer, my love.

Note to Readers

God's To-Do List presents Jewish wisdom for all people of faith. The biblical sources are drawn from two translations of the Five Books of Moses: *Etz Hayim: Torah and Commentary*, edited by David L. Lieber (Philadelphia: Jewish Publication Society, 2001) and *The Five Books of Moses*, translated by Everett Fox (New York: Schocken, 1995). I avoid masculine pronouns for God in my own writing, but have left biblical citations true to the original translations.

Introduction

I. God's To-Do List

God has a To-Do List for you.

"For me?"

Yes. For *you.*

You are God's partner.

God needs you to continue the ongoing creation of the world.

"What? Who? Me? I am God's *partner*?"

Yes. You are.

Because you are made in the image of God.

It says so, right at the beginning of the Bible:

> *And God made human beings in the image of God, male and female, God created them.*
>
> GENESIS 1:27

"Wait a minute. What does it mean to be 'made' in the 'image' of God?"

It means that the spark of divinity is within you.

And that God brought you into this world for a purpose.

The *ultimate* purpose.

This is it:

Your purpose is to do God's work.

The question has been asked:

What on earth are you here for?

The answer:

To do the tasks that God has for you.

Some faith traditions call this repairing the world.

Some call it bringing God's Kingdom to earth as it is in heaven.

"Whoa! That's Mother Teresa stuff! I'm no saint. It's not within my power to solve the big problems of the world."

Maybe not. But …

You can call someone who is lonely.

You can visit a friend who is sick.

You can read a book to a child.

You can comfort a mourner.

You can volunteer your time.

You can make a difference.

You can give of your self—a self that is infused with godliness.

Whatever your faith, you can do God's To-Do List.

God Needs You

"Excuse me? Would you repeat that, please?"

God needs you.

It's true that the God of the Bible is a God who is all-powerful, all-knowing—a real miracle worker.

Yet, even God realized that the world would need a very special presence, human beings who are literally infused with the breath—the spirit—of God to be the frontline caretakers of creation.

God can't do it alone. That's why God created you.

"Doesn't God have angels to help out?"

Yes, but …

God doesn't depend on angels.

God depends on you to be an angel.

> God doesn't depend on angels.
>
> God depends on you to be an angel.

As unbelievable as it may sound, you are God's agent on earth.

You are God's hands, feet, eyes, ears—and, most important, God's heart.

God needs you.

And when you perform an act of kindness, no matter how small, you bring God's presence into the world, into *your* world.

God has a To-Do List—for *you*.

In God's Image

It may be the most important verse in the Bible, so let me repeat it:

And God made human beings in the image of God, male and female, God created them.

GENESIS 1:27

Are you a reflection—an image—of God?

How do you look in the morning?

Let me tell you what I look like in the morning. I wake up and walk into the bathroom. I look into the mirror. My hair is usually standing straight up from my scalp in a thousand directions, my face is puffy, sleep still encrusted in the corners of my eyes. I stand there in my disheveled pajamas, looking like anything but a strong, competent, successful person. I haven't yet put on my glasses, so the image is kind of blurry ... but I know it's me.

Or is it?

What is the real reflection in the mirror?

Who am I?

Who are you?

"This is getting pretty deep."

Stay with me here.

Does the mirror reflect me—the many me's—spouse, friend, teacher, neighbor?

Or, is it me—a human being, made in the image of God?

The mirror does not belong to me.

Like all things on this earth, I only own it temporarily.

The mirror belongs to God.

And the reflection in it belongs to God, too.

When I look into a mirror, whom do I see?

I, like you, am made in God's image (*b'tzelem Elohim* in Hebrew), shaped to be God's agent on this earth, to be God's partner in shepherding it, repairing it, loving it. Becoming God's image and doing God's work is the ultimate purpose of my life—and it is the ultimate purpose of yours, too.

The next time you look in a mirror, ask yourself this question:

When I look into a mirror, whom do I see?

The Image in the Mirror

I want you to do something. Look into a mirror right now.

"Do I have to?"

Try it. If you don't have a mirror with you, find one. This little exercise could change the way you look at yourself and others forever!

Look carefully at your face. Look under your nose. Do you see that little indentation?

It is called the philtrum. Everyone has one.

"Okay. What is its purpose?"

Two thousand years ago, a teacher, Rabbi Bunim, asked the same question. With creative imagination and deep insight, the teacher gave this explanation:

> *While you are still in your mother's womb, God sends an angel to sit*
> *beside you to teach you all the wisdom you'll ever need to know to be*
> *God's partner on earth. Then, just before you are born, the angel taps you*
> *under the nose, forming the philtrum, the indentation that every human*
> *being has. And you forget everything the angel taught you!*
>
> TALMUD NIDDAH 30B

So, even though the spark of divinity is within you, you must relearn how to live a sacred life. Every time you look into a mirror and see the indentation right under your nose, you are reminded that not only are you *touched* by an angel, but you also have the potential to *be* an angel.

"What am I supposed to do when I look in the mirror and see an overworked and tired human being, burdened with worries, racked with self-doubt, and paralyzed by feelings of powerlessness?"

Here's what I do: I reach into my pockets. Two pockets.

There is a tradition that teaches to keep two slips of paper with you always, one in each pocket. Written on one is this quote from the Bible:

> *I am but dust and ashes.*
>
> GENESIS 18:27

These words are on the other slip of paper:

> *For my sake the world was created.*
>
> SANHEDRIN 37A

"Wait a minute. First, you tell me that I am made in the image of God. Then, you tell me that I am but dust and ashes. Now, you're telling me that the whole world was created for me? What's up with that? Which is it? Who am I?"

The two slips of paper serve different purposes. When you are full of yourself, riding high, in that nobody-can-top-me-now moment, one slip reminds you that, in the end—like all humans—you have limited time on this earth and you will, no question about it, return to dust and ash.

In one of his sermons, author John Ortberg uses a powerful metaphor to illustrate this reality. Remember playing the board game Monopoly? As a child, Ortberg loved to challenge his grandmother to a game. His grandmother was the kind of person who did not let children win at competitions in order to toughen them up, so she won all the time … until John learned the strategies necessary to save and spend money wisely, to buy properties and dominate the board. One day, one glorious day, John finally beat his grandmother at Monopoly. But, she had one more lesson to impart to him as John proudly surveyed all that he had acquired:

"Now it all goes back in the box."

It's true. All the things in this world belong to God.

The earth is the Lord's and all its fullness thereof …

PSALM 24:1

You just get to use God's stuff for a while. No matter how much you accumulate, it's not yours. Burial shrouds have no pockets. It all goes back in the box.

"I get it. It's like when my mother says, 'You can't take it with you.'"

Exactly. But, whenever you feel down, the tradition says to look at the slip of paper in your other pocket: *"For my sake the world was created."* It makes you feel like the most important person in the world. Understand its deeper meaning, though. Rick Warren, author of *The Purpose-Driven Life,* points out that it doesn't mean that everything in the world was created to *serve us;* it means human beings were created for *service.* Each person has a unique role to play, a particular set of gifts and abilities to make a difference in the world. No one else can make your contribution but you. You may be only one person in the world, but you may also be the world to one person.

You matter.

"Being responsible for a whole world is a pretty tall order."

Yes, but don't be overwhelmed. All God really wants you to do is to understand your real purpose and act on it. There is a saying:

> *The day is short and the task is great. It is not up to you to complete the work, but get in there, because you are not free to desist from it.*
> *SAYINGS OF THE ANCESTORS 2:15–16*

You have a choice. You can look into that mirror and see a cowering mammal. Or, you can look into that mirror and see a purposeful human being, made by God to be a steward of the earth and all its fullness thereof. The difference between feeling like a lump of dust and feeling as if the whole word was created for you depends on whether you can activate the spark of divinity within—and tackle God's To-Do List.

On the opposite page, you will find the two verses:

> *I am but dust and ashes.*
> *For my sake the world was created.*

Copy the page. Cut along the perforation line and put each in one of your pockets, or your purse, or your wallet.

I AM BUT DUST AND ASHES

....

FOR MY SAKE THE
WORLD WAS CREATED

Mirror Images

Consider the very first words of God's Original Top Ten To-Do List—the Ten Commandments: "I the Lord am your God ..." The Hebrew word for *your* is *Elohekha*, the singular form. Wouldn't it have made more sense for God to have said *your* in the plural? After all, God was addressing the To-Do List to the entire People Israel—six hundred thousand in number—assembled at the foot of Mount Sinai. The Rabbis noticed this and explained the reason:

> *God is like a mirror. The mirror never changes, but everyone who looks at it sees a different face. A thousand may look at it and it reflects each of them. Thus, the text does not say, "I the Lord am your God," addressed to the collective, but "I the Lord am your God," addressed to the individual.*
>
> P'SIKTA D'RAV KAHANA 12

God's mirror is one, but the reflections in it are many. Each one of us looks into God's mirror and sees a particular individual reflection of God.

"It's still hard for me to get my head around this. Some days, the last thing I think of myself as is an 'image of God.'"

> You are an image of God, put on this earth to do God's work.

But that's what you are.

You are an image of God, put on this earth to do God's work.

Discovering how to be God's image, how to kindle the spark of God in you, how to live a godly life, how to become God's partner in the ongoing work of creating the world and repairing its brokenness—this is the task of the spiritual journey ahead.

II. Be Like God

Do you remember Michael Jordan, one of the greatest basketball players ever? He was superhuman. He made miraculous shots. He was idolized by millions.

At the height of his popularity, there was a TV commercial targeted mainly to young people who aspired to be as successful, as powerful, as awe-inspiring as him—their role model—Michael Jordan.

"Wasn't it for Gatorade—that sports drink?"

Correct. The tag line was "Be Like Mike." And how can you be like Mike?

You drink Gatorade.

The Bible teaches: *Be Like God.*

"How can you be like God?"

Let God be your role model.

Let God be your role model.

Be Holy

The most important commandment in the Bible is not in God's Original To-Do List. It comes in Leviticus, in the code of laws and instructions that God gives through Moses to the People Israel. Here it is:

> *You shall be holy, because I, the Lord your God, am holy.*
>
> LEVITICUS 19:1–2

"Just a second. What does it mean to be *holy*? I know how to be nice. I know how to be loyal. I know how to be honest. I'm not sure I know how to be *holy.*"

That's the deal. God wants you to be holy, because you are made in God's image, and if God is holy, you—God's reflection—should be holy.

After God calls the people to be holy, the Bible details how to be holy in virtually all areas of living:

Honor your parents.

Observe the Sabbath.

Don't create idols.

Be careful what you eat.

Leave some of your food for the poor.

Be kind.

And it continues from there, listing law after law about family, the cycle of the year, business dealings, and relationships between neighbors.

Biblical scholars call these chapters The Holiness Code.

It is one way to learn how to be holy.

But, there's another way to holiness.

In addition to hearing what God says, you can observe what God does. In fact, God says as much in the Bible:

> *Follow Adonai [Yahweh] your God …*
>
> DEUTERONOMY 13:5

"What does it mean to *follow* God?"

Walk in God's footsteps.

"But, it's not possible for a human being to walk in the footsteps of God."

Follow the *acts* of God, Holy One of Blessing.

How can you be holy?

Be like God.

Behave like God.

Do God's To-Do List.

Acts of God

Do you have insurance on your home?

"Yes."

When the hurricanes blow or the earth moves, have you ever heard someone say, "It was an act of God?"

"Sure."

> In addition to hearing what God says, you can observe what God does.

Well, your insurance company protects you against human-made mistakes, but not "acts of God." God gets a bad rap. A better term for disasters would be "acts of nature."

God does acts of good.

The Bible is filled with instances of how God acts in relationship with human beings made in the divine image. Here are just a few:

God clothes the naked.

When Adam and Eve are in the Garden of Eden and eat of the Tree of Knowledge, they realize they are naked and become embarrassed. God performs an act of kindness to save them from embarrassment. "And the Lord God made for Adam and for his wife garments of skins and clothed them" (Gen. 3:21).

God attends the bride.

When Adam and Eve are married, who makes the wedding? They have no human parents! Nevertheless, in the vibrant imagination of early biblical commentators, there is a wedding. Who is Adam's best man? God. One commentator adds a beautiful image to the scene: before she is married, God braids Eve's hair (*Brachot* 61a)!

God visits the sick.

When Abraham enters into a relationship with God, he is instructed (Gen. 17:24) to mark the covenant by circumcising himself at the ripe-old age of ninety-nine years! The very next scene in the Bible describes Abraham sitting in the entrance of his tent. "The Lord appeared to him by the terebinths of Mamre; he was sitting at the entrance of his tent as the day grew hot" (Gen. 18:1). The Talmudic commentator (*Sotah* 14a) cites this as the first example of God visiting the sick, the gift of a caring presence.

God comforts the mourner.

"After the death of Abraham, God blessed his son Isaac" (Gen. 25:11). This is the first instance of God comforting a mourner.

God feeds the hungry.

When the Israelites wander in the desert for forty years, what do they eat? God provides manna (Exod. 16:4).

God buries the dead.

Moses, God's great partner in the miraculous liberation of the Israelites from Egypt, dies alone. Unlike Abraham and Sarah, who are buried in the Cave of Machpelah, or Rachel, who is buried in a tomb near Bethlehem, there is no account of precisely where Moses is buried. Who does this last act of kindness, an act for which one can never be repaid?

God buries Moses. "So Moses the servant of the Lord died there, in the land of Moab, at the command of the Lord [literally, "by the mouth of the Lord," meaning God reclaimed his soul by kissing him (*Mo'ed Katan* 28a)]. And God buried him in the valley in the land of Moab" (Deut. 34:6).

"That's all well and good. Thank you for the Bible lesson. But what does it have to do with me?"

It has everything to do with you. Because you are God's partner on earth. So, just as God clothes the naked, *you* are to clothe the naked.

Just as God visits the sick, *you* are to visit the sick.

Just as God comforts the mourner, *you* are to comfort the mourner.

Just as God attends the bride, *you* are to attend the bride.

Just as God feeds the hungry, *you* are to feed the hungry.

Just as God buries the dead, *you* are to bury the dead.

Imitate God's acts of good and you join forces with the Divine to create a better world. It's the way human beings become as close as possible to being one with God.

Item Number One on God's To-Do List

Look again at the To-Do that forms the basis for everything else. This is item Number One on God's Original Top Ten To-Do List:

> *I am the Lord your God who brought you out of the Land of Egypt, the house of bondage: You shall have no other gods but Me.*
>
> EXODUS 20:2–3

This made sense to a people who had just come from idol-laden Egypt and who had made a Golden Calf. This To-Do is all about recognizing the Oneness of God. That's what it means to be a monotheist—in the Christian, Jewish, and Muslim traditions, there is only one God.

Yet, many people serve other gods.

The god of money. The god of fashion. The god of beauty. The god of work. The god of celebrity.

You've got a To-Do List from God.

Do any of these things rule your life?

If they do, the To-Do here is to believe in one God and stop idolizing these other things. Do what God put you on earth to do. For Jews, it is to follow God's footsteps and repair the world to bring God's presence on earth. For Christians, it is to follow the way of Jesus and build the Kingdom. For Muslims, it is to follow the laws of Muhammad to bring justice and peace in the name of Allah.

You've got a To-Do List from God.

III. Doing God's To-Do List

Ask What You Can Do

When John F. Kennedy was elected president of the United States, he gave one of the truly great inaugural addresses in history, a speech that resonates to this day. The best-known line from his January 20, 1961, Inaugural Address was his call to action:

> And so my fellow Americans, ask not what your country can do for you; ask what you can do for your country.

He could have stopped there, but he didn't. Kennedy ended his speech by giving the *reason* to ask what you can do:

> With a good conscience our only sure reward, with history the final judge of our deeds, let us go forth to lead the land we love, asking His blessing and His help, but knowing that here on earth God's work must truly be our own.

This book is about how God's work here on earth must truly be your own. It's about asking yourself what you can do as God's partner.

Go Forth

President Kennedy's call to "go forth" echoes the biblical call from God to Abraham and Sarah:

> *Go forth from your native land, from your father's house....*
>
> GENESIS 12:1

In other words, you're about to embark on a journey.

If there is one master metaphor in the Bible, it is the notion of journey. Think of all the journeys the central characters take. Adam and Eve, Noah, Abraham and Sarah, Jacob, Joseph, Moses—they all are called by God to take significant journeys.

How do you take a journey?

Have you ever planned a trip?

"Of course."

God's work here on earth must truly be your own.

Where did you get information?

"The Internet, guidebooks, recommendations from friends."

Do you belong to AAA?

I do. I carry my AAA membership card in my wallet. It says I've been a member for thirty-six years. In all that time, I have used the card only for roadside services—once when I had a flat tire and three times when the battery went dead. Until one day, when visiting our family in Omaha, Nebraska, on our way to take our daughter Havi to the University of Michigan, I needed a map to Ann Arbor. I remembered my AAA card. So I went into the local office, and the experience changed my life.

When I walked into the AAA office, I was warmly greeted at a reception desk. I showed my membership card to the receptionist and asked for a map from Omaha to Ann Arbor.

"Well," the receptionist said, "we can certainly get you a map, but wouldn't you like to meet with someone and really plan your trip?"

I was in no particular hurry and agreed.

Within minutes, I was escorted to a counter and introduced to Steve, my personal counselor.

"Hi. I'm Steve, how can I help you?"

"I'm going from Omaha to Ann Arbor ... "

"Great," Steve replied, and he pulled out a huge map of the United States and used a yellow marker to highlight a path from Omaha to Ann Arbor to give me the big picture of the journey.

"Thanks," I said, and prepared to leave with my map.

"Wait a second," he stopped me. "Let me show you this."

Steve pulled out a map of the Central States Region and began the same drill, marking a route from Omaha to Ann Arbor with that yellow marker. I noticed this map had more information than the first map.

"Thanks," I said, and prepared to leave with my second map.

Oh no. Steve had something else up his sleeve.

"Now that we have an overview," Steve smiled, "I'm going to make you a TripTik."

"A what?" I asked.

Steve began to pull together a whole series of small strip maps of the route he had outlined on the large map and the regional map. Each strip map showed at most one hundred fifty miles between points along the way.

The TripTik maps were very different from the larger maps of the United States. There was much greater detail; there were notes about the terrain ("soft, rolling fields of corn becoming grazing for livestock in the east"). On the back, there were even brief descriptions of points of interest along the way.

I noticed that just south of Des Moines, Iowa, the road led to Madison County.

I couldn't help but ask Steve: "Is that *the* Madison County?"

Steve laughed. "Yep. My wife made me read that book, too!"

"Can you actually visit the bridges of Madison County?"

"Yep. My wife dragged me there a couple of years ago. They are fabulously romantic. My wife loved them. If you have time, you should stop there. You want a map?"

Steve continued through my itinerary, pulling out map after map, and then, to top it all off, he produced two thick tour books, the kind with the descriptions of sites, listings of accommodations, and things to do on the journey. By the time our forty-five minute consultation was over, I had a sack full of maps, tour books, and my personalized TripTik. I left the AAA office feeling excited and confident about taking the journey.

Like cross-country trips, spiritual journeys are taken one step at a time.

Think of your life as a walk with God.

At the conclusion of the Book of Leviticus, God promises that if you follow God's laws and faithfully observe God's commandments—To-Dos— God will bring abundant blessings (Lev. 26:3–13). The Hebrew word for follow is *taileikhu*, literally, "you shall walk."

Do one small To-Do every day.

How do you walk with God?

Put one foot in front of the other—and begin.

You will have many opportunities to do God's work along your journey, to walk in God's ways, to make a difference in God's world. Do the items on God's To-Do List one at a time.

Do one small To-Do every day.

When you do, God will smile on you.

How to Do This Book

Did you notice I am about to describe how *to do* this book, not how to read it?

"Yes, very clever, Ron."

I want you to engage this book, to interact with it, to *do it*.

That's the purpose of the book—to inspire you to do God's To-Do List. *Your* God's To-Do List.

Here's how to do this book:

1. *Read the chapters.*

   There are ten chapters, and each one contains examples of one of the acts of good that God does in the Bible beginning at the beginning. What is the very first thing God does? God creates the universe. So, chapter one is called "Create." If God creates, you can create—because you have the spark of divinity within you, and God wants you to use your talent and skill to create. I also tell some stories of how human beings can be creative.

2. *Consider the 103 items on God's To-Do List.*

   At the end of each chapter, I offer ten ways to live your purpose and do God's work on earth. They vary from very simple things you can do every day to complex projects that could take a long time to achieve. You might not be able to do all the To-Dos I suggest because of your unique life situation. These ideas are meant to be an example for you, to stimu- late you to think about what is possible.

3. *Think of what God is calling you to do.*

   At the end of God's To-Do List in each chapter, there are blank spaces. I invite you to pause in your reading and reflect on what God is calling you to do. If God made a To-Do List for you, tailored to your God-given talents and skills that can be used to make a difference in the world, what would be on the list? Write down a few of the To-Dos, either on a separate sheet of paper or in the book itself.

4. *Compile your very own God's To-Do List.*

   When you have finished reading the book, go back to the To-Do Lists at the end of each chapter. Pick out one or two of the items that best resonate with who you are, where you are on your life journey, and what you can really commit to doing. Copy the template for "My God's

To-Do List" at the end of the book. Write your name on the top. Fill it out. Put this first list on your refrigerator, your bulletin board, near your bedstand, on your closet door, on your bathroom mirror, in your car, next to the remote control, on your computer monitor—some place where you will see the list every day.

5. *Now, do your To-Dos.*

6. *Keep track.*

When you do a To-Do, put a check mark next to the item, not to check it off, but to document for yourself how you are doing, doing God's work.

7. *Revisit, revise, refresh.*

Once you begin to see yourself, and the other human beings around you, as a partner with God, everything changes. You will look at the world differently. As you do, revisit, revise, and refresh your God's To-Do Lists. Who knows where the journey will take you? Who knows what God will call you to do? Only you will know. Give yourself permission to grow as the godliness within you emerges.

8. *Share your God's To-Do List.*

When someone—your child, your spouse, your friend—asks you about your God's To-Do List, tell him or her about it. Share your feelings about being a partner with God in making the world a better place. Perhaps your congregation will have a small group of people doing To-Dos together. Join them!

9. *Read your list.*

Take the time to read your list. Every day. As you do God's work, recognize who you are becoming. Let the work you are doing now inspire you to even greater service.

10. *If you get stuck, read this.*

How wonderful it is that nobody need wait a single moment before beginning to improve the world.

ANNE FRANK

Be an Angel

What happens when you do something on God's To-Do List?

You become an angel.

Has anyone ever asked you to "be an angel"?

It's a common figure of speech:

"Be an angel and watch the kids for an hour while I run to the store."

"Honey, on your way home, be an angel and pick up the dry-cleaning."

Sometimes, you are called on to be an angel for things far more serious.

When you call or visit your elderly parent every day, you're being an angel.

If you organize some friends to do volunteer work in the community, you're being an angel.

By saying an encouraging word to a child who is down, you're being an angel.

You have the potential to be an angel.

Every human being on earth can be an angel.

So, when someone does something wonderful for you, don't forget to say thank you. You're thanking an angel.

Be a Blessing

When you act like an angel, you are a blessing.

You are a blessing to those whom you help.

And, you are a blessing to yourself.

"How can that be? How can you be a blessing to *yourself*?"

God says you can.

In fact, in the Bible, God actually calls you to be a blessing.

Remember the call to Abraham and Sarah to "go forth"? God doesn't tell them where exactly they are going, but, if they go, God makes a promise— a *big* promise:

> *I will make of you a great nation,*
> *And I will bless you;*
> *I will make your name great,*
> *And you shall be a blessing.*

GENESIS 12:2

Listen to God's call.
Be an angel.
Do God's To-Do List.
And you will be a blessing.

1
Create

God is very creative.

If the Bible is a biography of God, isn't it curious that there is no account of how God came to be? Depending on your translation, the opening line is:

> *In the beginning God created the heavens and the earth … (NIV)*

or

> *When God began to create heaven and earth … (JPS)*

or

> *At the beginning of God's creating of the heavens and earth … (Fox)*

Notice that God is not created. God's existence is assumed.

We quickly learn the first characteristic of God: God creates.

In rapid succession, God creates the heavens and the earth, light, darkness, sky, earth, sun, and moon; creatures of the sea, sky, and land; and humankind.

How does God create?

With *words*.

> *God said: "Let there be light"; and there was light.*

> GENESIS 1:3

God the Creator *calls* the world into being.

Once something is created, God *perceives* it and *assesses* it:

God's ultimate creations—human beings—are endowed with this same capacity to create.

21

God saw that the light was good …

GENESIS 1:4

Then, God *names* the creation:

God called the light Day …

GENESIS 1:5

The act of creation, then, begins with intention—often expressed in words, creating something, looking at it, judging it, naming it, and—ultimately—documenting and remembering it.

God's ultimate creations—human beings—are endowed with this same capacity to create.

The Gift of Creating

Samuel Morse was a creator. He intended to create a method of communication between human beings over long distances. There had been other methods of speaking to each other: smoke signals, tom-toms, bonfires on mountaintops, and torches. But these had very limited range. Morse wanted to use his knowledge of physics and electricity to invent an apparatus to enable communication over long distances. After nine years of trial and error, he finally succeeded in sending a message from Washington to Baltimore. It read:

What hath God wrought?

Morse, a partner with God in creation, knew that this was very good.
He named his invention the telegraph.
It changed the world.

Sometimes, inspiration drives creativity.

My father, Alan, is a sometimes inventor. A dental technician in World War II, he dreamed for years of inventing a new kind of toothbrush, one that would brush both sides of the teeth simultaneously. He thought it would be useful for children, the elderly, and even dogs. He played with numerous ideas, but none of them really worked. Then, one day, he experienced a flash of inspiration while watching a custodian polish the floor in a shopping mall. He reasoned that a circular brush, like the one on the floor polisher, would do a much better job cleaning the teeth and gums than the standard rectangular brush. By putting two small circular brushes facing each other, you could brush both sides of the teeth at the same time!

To tell the truth, the first prototype of Dad's toothbrush hardly evoked aha's. In fact, most people who saw it reacted with ha-ha's. It didn't help that he crudely fashioned the two brushes on the end of a plastic water pistol, which looked pretty scary when he stuck it in his mouth to demonstrate! Undaunted, he went to an inventors fair in a small Nebraska town, someone saw the potential, manufactured a version of the toothbrush, one thing led to another, and two years later, a major company produced the Fpi-dent Rotary Toothbrush, based on U.S. Patent 346732879, held by Alan Wolfson, my dad. When he saw his toothbrush being sold in Bloomingdale's in his native New York City, you would have thought he had just won the Nobel Prize.

Liz Lerman is an extraordinarily creative human being. A dancer and choreographer, Liz has created a nonprofit organization dedicated to practicing the art of dance in its fullest range of functions—as a way to learn, heal, and comprehend the universe, as a performing art on stages around the world, and as a way of organizing and celebrating community. Liz and her troupe—the Liz Lerman Dance Exchange—take up residence in communities and link partners, such as a dance performance space and a prison, a civic center and a senior center, a hospital and a dance festival.

Liz is gifted at using the art of dance and story to enable those who do not necessarily think of themselves as dancers to share personal experiences and ideas. Through community workshops, people from all walks of life discover their capacity to dance and to express themselves through movement. Workshop participants then create a performance she calls a "community participation dance."

Liz believes that no one is too old or too young to dance. With incredible skill, she and her colleagues encourage people who would never in a million years think of themselves as dancers to engage in the creative process of dance.

Imagine, hundreds of people in Portsmouth, New Hampshire, celebrating their two hundred-year-old history in a dance held in the city's naval shipyard! Imagine, a large-scale celebration of the millennium called "The Hallelujah Project," which brought community-based dance performances to cities across America. Imagine, docents and members of a Jewish museum interpreting through dance an exhibit called "The History of Matzah." Imagine, a troupe of dancers moving among the musicians in a symphony orchestra. Imagine participating in a process of sharing personal story, retrieving rituals from the past, and listening to young people envision their futures—all to create an experience called "Prayer as a Radical Act/Radical Action as Prayer."

The latest exploration by Liz is mind-boggling in its creativity. She is currently developing a multimedia work about what's going on in the laboratories of genetic science and what impact this will have on our lives. How we eat, how we heal, how we age, how we procreate—today's scientific culture will deeply affect all these things, and perhaps more quickly than we think. The project is fostering a long-term partnership among a national group of scientists, bioethicists, researchers, clergy, and artists, who will bring their best thinking to bear on the promise and threat of a new biological age. The piece is called "Ferocious Beauty: Genome."

In 2002, Liz Lerman was honored as a MacArthur "Genius" Fellow for her creativity. A treasure trove of her creative techniques can be found in her toolbox at www.danceexchange.org/toolbox/.

Once, while browsing in an antique store, a small embroidered pillow in the shape of a heart caught my attention. Stitched onto the front of the pillow were these words:

Moms Make Memories

I bought it immediately and gave it to my wife, Susie, as a present, for her God-given talents have blessed our family with a lifetime of precious memories.

For the thirty-six years we've been married and the thirty years we have had children, Susie has been an extraordinarily creative home and memory maker. She transformed our daily meals into experiences, our holidays into theme parties, and our life-cycle events into meaningful celebrations.

A few years ago, she went to a wedding shower where every guest was asked to bring a recipe. The hosts put together the recipes in a book for the bride-to-be, a lovely idea. When the groom's mother flipped through the recipes, her eye caught one for tuna fish salad. It called for yogurt instead of mayonnaise. The groom's mother couldn't help herself and she blurted out: "Yogurt in tuna fish?! My son won't eat yogurt in tuna fish!"

At that moment, Susie had an epiphany. All these guests had brought foreign recipes to the bride. Neither she nor her groom would be familiar with them, because they hadn't grown up with the dishes created by the recipes. Wouldn't it make more sense for the new bride to have recipes for the foods and meals that her groom was used to?

Susie then and there decided that she would write down the recipes she had created and used for our favorite family meals and collect recipes from other family members who bring their specialties to our celebrations.

Susie did much more than transcribe the recipes. She created page upon page of recipes embellished with photos of the people who contributed the recipes and stories about the dish or the meal: Havi's favorite Chinese chicken salad, Michael's favorite "eggies in a hole," Aunt Rose's Jell-O mold, cousin Margo's mandel bread.

The title of the book is *Recipes for Memories*. It's not a memoir. It's not a cookbook. It's not a scrapbook.

It is the story of our family.

When Susie finished this incredible project, she presented a copy to each of our young adult children. Havi took one look at it and broke down in tears of memory and gratitude. Michael, a hipster and rock music maven, flipped through the pages in amazement and said: "Wow! This is my life!!!" and proceeded to read every word on every page.

The real payoff came the next Passover holiday. Susie always sends Michael a care package of holiday foods and objects before the major

Jewish holidays, with the hope that it will encourage him to have some kind of celebration if he's not visiting us. Michael called to thank us for the package. "Mom, Dad ... it was great that you included the matzah ball mix. I actually made some ... and I used your cookbook, Mom!" I thought Susie was going to fall off her chair when she heard that!

You see, in our family, we have a matzah ball battle that would rival anything on *Iron Chef*. Matzah balls are a kind of dumpling made from matzah (unleavened bread) and eggs. My mom, Michael's grandmother, who in our family is known as Bubbie W. (*Bubbie* is a Yiddish term of endearment), makes big, fluffy, soft matzah balls that float in a bowl of soup. Susie's dad, aka Zadie K. (*Zadie* is the Yiddish word for "grandfather"), makes golf-ball-size hard matzah balls that sink to the bottom of the bowl. In *Recipes for Memories*, Susie created a page with both recipes, a page she titled "Dueling Matzah Balls."

When Michael revealed that he had actually made matzah balls using the cookbook, Susie could hardly contain her curiosity and asked, "Which recipe did you use to make the matzah balls? How did they come out?"

Michael calmly replied: "Well, I was going for Bubbie, but they came out Zadie!"

Sharing Your Spark of Divinity

God is the Creator.

You can be a creator, too.

The Bible is God's memory book. It contains the stories of God's family as they journeyed through life. It details the "recipes" for how to be God's partner in the world. It records for all time God's To-Do Lists.

When you create, you're releasing your godliness into the world.

God is the Creator.

You can be a creator, too.

God's To-Do List

 Create

1. Use your God-given gift of creativity—paint, draw, sculpt, photograph, compose, dance, write, cook, bake.

2. Collect evidence of your "creations"—your children, your achievements, your experiences, your journeys—by creating memory scrapbooks to document them, and take pleasure in your creations.

3. Create a CD of your favorite songs, a website, or a blog (online journal).

4. Learn a new skill to use for your creative endeavors, like knitting or calligraphy.

5. Use creativity techniques to broaden your horizons—brainstorm, think outside the box, free-associate.

6. Surround yourself with creative people, creative environments, and creative experiences.

7. Create a new relationship—make a friend, be a Big Brother or a Big Sister (see www.bbbs.org).

8. Gather friends and create a community mural to brighten a neighborhood.

9. "Be fruitful and multiply"—create a bigger family by adopting or having children, or by taking in a foster child.

10. Create a nonprofit organization or activity to support a cause that inspires you.

2
Bless

"God bless you."

It is a common phrase. You say it all the time.

Usually when someone sneezes.

From the very beginning, God blesses. It's the second thing God does in the Bible.

In the creation story, God blesses three times:

1. God blesses the living creatures and birds, saying: "Be fertile and increase, fill the waters in the seas, and let the birds increase on earth" (Gen. 1:22).
2. God blesses humans. "God blessed them and God said to them: 'Be fertile and increase, fill the earth and master it; and rule the fish of the sea, the birds of the sky, and all the living things that creep on the earth'" (Gen. 1:28).
3. God blesses the Sabbath. "And God blessed the seventh day and declared it holy, because on it God ceased from all the work of creation that God created to do" (Gen. 2:3)

In the first instance, God blesses the animals and birds with the ability to reproduce. It seems as if God offers the same blessing to human beings, except there is a major difference. Unlike with the animals, God addresses human beings *directly:* "God blessed them and God said to them." This establishes the intimate connection between God and humans that will characterize their relationship throughout the Bible.

The divine blessings continue throughout the Bible. God blesses Abraham as he begins his journey. God blesses Sarah with a child. God blesses Isaac after his father dies.

Three Ways of Blessing

How can you fill your life with blessings?
There are three ways.

Bless Some Thing or Some Action

Have you ever wanted to do something and you wanted someone's *blessing* to do it?

Perhaps you asked your boss for permission to try a new approach to solving a problem. "I'd like to try this. Do I have your blessing?"

Or it could be something more personal. A young man who has fallen in love with your daughter asks you for her hand in marriage: "I am asking for your blessing."

We were ready to give our blessing to a guy who fell in love with our daughter. Havi had met Sam (not his real name) on a popular Internet dating site; he looked perfect on paper. He was a thirty-two-year-old dentist, lived nearby, never-married, tall, handsome—and Jewish. Their relationship began with e-mails, but within a week, they arranged to meet for a coffee date. When Sam saw Havi in person, he said: "Forget coffee. We're going to dinner." This is known as an "instant upgrade."

Havi and Sam quickly became attached. He was real potential. Things looked very, very promising. Sam was charming, paid for everything, and even took Havi to his synagogue for services. Gifts were exchanged, the parents met, and Sam became a fixture in our home. Month after month went by and we began to ask Havi: "So, *nu*? When will he ask you to marry him?" We were convinced the engagement was around the corner. Young people today certainly take their time.

We liked Sam and he liked us. He even offered to be our dentist. I was ready; Susie freaked out. "No way he's putting his hands in my mouth," she said. "Too weird." But, I went, he did a good job, and he charged the family rate. I encouraged Susie to go, and eventually she gave in.

You know how when you go to a new doctor's office for the first time, they give you a form to fill out with all your information? On Susie's first visit to Dr. Sam, nearly a year after Havi had met him, she got the form and sat down in the waiting room to fill it out. The first line was: "Name _____"; Susie wrote in

"Susan Wolfson." The second line was: "Name I Prefer to be Called
_____"; Susie wrote in "Mom."

The good doctor never noticed it, or pretended not to; he never said a word. We should have known it was a sign. Sam never asked us for our blessing—and that should have been a sign, too. Eventually, he gave her a ring and things went downhill from there. Sam turned out not to be the nice guy we all thought he was, and Havi did one of the most courageous acts imaginable—she broke off the engagement. She's dating a great guy now, and we're hopeful he *will* ask for our blessing should the time come.

Count Your Blessings

The second way to fill your life with blessing is to count your blessings. When do you count your blessings?

In the classic film *White Christmas*, Bing Crosby sings an Academy Award–nominated song, "Count Your Blessings," written by Irving Berlin. The words suggest that when you are feeling low—the bankroll is down, you're worried and can't sleep at night—think of the time you had "nothing at all" and remember the "curly heads" slumbering in their beds—and count your blessings.

It's good advice.

My nephew Avi was born with mitochondrial myopathy and cannot speak. A sweet, lovable, bear hug of a boy, Avi has been a challenge for my brother, Doug, and his wife, Sara. Against all odds, they refused to institutionalize Avi and have raised him beautifully along with his brother, Aaron, and sister, Naomi. When our family received an invitation to Avi's bar mitzvah, the time when thirteen-year-old Jewish children transition to "adult" status, we couldn't believe it! How could Avi lead the congregation in prayer? How could he recite from the Bible? How could he give the bar mitzvah speech?

When the big day arrived, the sanctuary was packed. Avi strode to the pulpit in his brand-new suit and awaited instructions from his teachers. The rabbi explained that, although Avi could not speak, he would lead the service by interpreting the prayers. Before singing the prayer thanking God for the blessings of creation, Avi walked to the middle of the pulpit and proudly held up a painting he had drawn depicting the creation of heaven and earth. Before the prayer recalling ancestors, Avi held up a poster he had made of his family tree. When it came time to read from the ancient scroll of the Torah, brother Aaron read while Avi followed along. For his bar mitzvah speech, Avi's mother said: "If Avi could speak, this is what he would say: 'Thank you to all of you for coming to share in my big day. Mom and Dad, sorry I got you up early this morning, but I was so excited. Aaron and Naomi, I love you, no matter what. To all my family, I keep photos of you near my bed and look at them every night. Thank you to my teachers for helping me prepare for this day. And, now remember, say "hi" to everyone like I do, hug everyone like I do, and love everyone like I do.'" There wasn't a dry eye in the place.

Then, when the last prayer was recited, a miracle happened! Avi said his first word: "Yesss!" We counted our blessings that day as Avi taught us the strength of a human soul.

Ask God's Blessings

Doug and Sara taught the congregation something else that morning— the third way we recognize the blessings in our lives—ask God's blessings for those we love.

When do you bless your children?

> You are God's partner, and you have the power to bless.

At Avi's bar mitzvah, instead of the usual long, flowery, parental speech about their child's prowess at soccer, school, piano, and shopping, Doug and Sara simply stood in front of Avi that morning and blessed him. They began by using sign language to say just three words to Avi: "We love you!" Then, as many Jewish parents do on every Sabbath and major holiday, Doug and Sara asked for God to bless their child. Parents recite the same blessing offered by the High Priest for the People Israel in ancient times:

> *May God bless you and watch over you.*
> *May God smile at you and offer you kindness beyond what you deserve.*
> *May God's presence be with you always, and may you enjoy the blessings of peace.*

> NUMBERS 6:24–26

There is something quite extraordinary about this.

This is the same blessing that clergy often recite at key life-cycle moments. If this is what priests and rabbis say, what right do parents have in offering it to their children?

God blesses you.

You can bless others.

The answer: every right.

You are God's partner, and you have the power to bless.

Daily Blessings

Say, "God bless you" when someone sneezes.

Say, "God bless you" to your loved ones on a regular basis.

God blesses you.

You can bless others.

God's To-Do List

 Bless

11. Bless your children and spouse.

12. Bless your extended family and your friends.

13. Bless your home. Make it a sanctuary, a safe place, a retreat.

14. Bless your country.

15. If someone gives you great service, ask the person for the name of her/his boss and write a thank-you note.

16. Ask God's blessings for the food you eat, safe journeys, and healing.

17. Ask your clergy to offer blessings from God at times of need.

18. When someone asks you for your blessing, give it.

19. Think of yourself as a blessing. You are!

20. Count your blessings. Start today. Copy the next page. Fill it out and put it somewhere you will see it—every day.

_____

_____

_____

_____

_____

_____

_____

God's To-Do List

  Count My Blessings

1. _____

2. _____

3. _____

4. _____

5. _____

6. _____

7. _____

8. _____

9. _____

10. _____

3
Rest

After six days of creating, God does something quite remarkable—remarkable for the all-powerful God of monotheistic religions.

God rests.

> *On the seventh day God finished the work that God had been doing, and God ceased on the seventh day from all the work that God had done. And God blessed the seventh day and declared it holy, because on it God ceased from all the work that God created to do.*
>
> GENESIS 2:2–3

Notice the text does not use the word *rest*; instead, it uses *cease*. The literal translation of the original Hebrew word—*shabbat*—is "cease," "stop." God stopped creating on the seventh day. Rest is a by-product of stopping the work of creating.

The biblical notion of a Sabbath day is one of the great gifts to humankind. It is so important that it is number four on God's Original Top Ten To-Do List:

> *Observe the Sabbath day and keep it holy.*
>
> DEUTERONOMY 5:12

Abraham Joshua Heschel, a great twentieth-century philosopher, wrote in his classic book *The Sabbath* (page 28):

> To set apart one day a week for freedom, a day on which we would not use the instruments which have been so easily turned into weapons of destruction, a day for being with ourselves, a day of detachment from the vulgar, a day on which we stop worshiping the idols of technical

civilization, a day of armistice in the economic struggle with our fellow men—is there any institution that holds out a greater hope for human progress than the Sabbath?

Rest—for Yourself, for Your Loved Ones

Fred was asked why he decided to observe the Sabbath. He said, simply: "I couldn't live without it. I have a whole twenty-four hours to spend time with my family and friends, pray in community, study a portion of the Bible, enjoy a leisurely meal, nap in the afternoon, and take a walk. Every week. Fifty-two weeks a year. By the time I am seventy years old, I will have enjoyed nearly *ten years* of Sabbath-time! *Ten years!*"

When I was a teenager, I learned a lesson about one of the true gifts of the Sabbath. Our family business in Omaha was Louis (pronounced Louie's) Market, a large grocery store in one building and a combination family bar/package liquor store in the other. It was founded by my grandfather, Louis Paperny, an immigrant from Russia who started his business peddling fruits and vegetables. When each of his four daughters married, Louie gave each of his sons-in-law an equal partnership in the business.

My dad, Alan the Inventor, worked incredibly long hours at the store, constantly on his feet, serving customers, stocking shelves, and managing the help. It was exhausting. The busiest time of the week was Friday night and Saturday. People got paid on Friday and the first thing they did was buy groceries.

Dad never worked on Friday night. The Jewish Sabbath begins at sundown Friday night and extends through Saturday sundown. My mother insisted on ushering in the Sabbath with the traditional ritual and meal, just as her mother had done when she was a child. All four of us men—sons Ronnie, Bobby, and Dougie, and Dad—were expected to be at the table. Even though Dad used to talk about how much he admired the famous agnostic Spinoza and he wasn't sure he believed in God, he dutifully acquiesced to Mom's commitment to the family dinner.

When I was in junior high school, I entered what can only be called the early adolescent rebellion stage of life. One Friday afternoon, I was hanging out with friends at the local shopping mall, having a great time, until I looked at my watch. It read seven-thirty. I was supposed to be home by six o'clock on Friday afternoon. I hopped on the bus and strolled into the house at eight. I knew I was in trouble, but I had no idea I was about to learn one of the most important lessons of my life.

Mom was on the phone with the police, hysterically crying, worried that I had been in an accident or shot. Dad saw me walk in, embraced me with a sigh of relief, and then turned angry: "Ronnie, where have you been!? You missed Shabbat dinner!"

I replied, as only an adolescent could, "So what, Dad? You don't believe in any of this religious stuff anyway!"

I can't exactly remember what happened next. But, when I woke up, my dad and I had one of those father-son talks that will stay with me forever.

"I am so disappointed in you, Ronnie," he began. "Your mother was frantic. We had no idea where you were, if you were in trouble—it's a terrible feeling. You know that we expect you to be at the dinner table on Friday night."

"I'm sorry, Dad," I mumbled. "I should have called you; I didn't realize what time it was. But I still don't get what's so important about Shabbat dinner."

"Let me explain something to you, son. I work like a dog, every day, all week long. I take off one night a week—Friday night. Not Saturday night, when all of our friends are out on the town. I never take off Saturday night; I take off Friday night. You know why? So, I can be with your mother and my boys for a meal, a meal that isn't rushed, a meal that's taken at the dining room table, not in front of the TV, a meal where I can sit and talk with you about school and your week. Then I kick off my shoes and we play a game or read a book. It's our family time. It's the best time of my week."

And then, for the first time in my life, my Dad cried in front of me.

His emotional words drilled through me, and suddenly I realized what was at stake for him. I understood his anger and disappointment in my casual dismissal of the importance of being home for this time. For him and my mother, who also worked out of the house, the Sabbath was not just a time for rest. By welcoming the Sabbath on a weekly basis, they sought to ensure quality time for us to be a family.

God knows, you need some rest.

In an era when everyone in the family is exhausted from school, work, lessons, sports, and endless carpools, time off just to be together is one of the greatest gifts you can give each other.

Put it on your God's To-Do List.

Restore Your Strength to Continue God's Work

Look carefully at this biblical passage again. Most translations of the Hebrew read:

> *"… God ceased from all the work of creation that God had done."*

The literal translation of the Hebrew is:

> *"… God ceased from all the work that God created to do."*

A biblical commentator from the Middle Ages, Ibn Ezra, explains that the use of the words *to do* indicates that the work of creation was not finished on the seventh day; rather, God completed setting up the basic structures of the world that God's partners would then be responsible for. Thus, the translation should read:

> *"God ceased from all the work that God created (for human beings) to continue doing."*

God depends on human beings, made in the image of God, to continue the work of creation. Just as God stopped the initial work of creation on the seventh day, so you are to take a break from the ongoing work of creating, to refresh and renew yourself for the week ahead.

God knows, you need some rest.

Aren't you exhausted at the end of the workweek?

If God took a break from creating, shouldn't you?

God depends on you to continue the work of creation the other six days of the week.

Take a day off.

Rest up.

Take a day off.

God's To-Do List

 Rest

21. Give yourself a break. Take a day off once a week.

22. Put aside your unfinished business and leave the world as it is on the Sabbath.

23. Turn off the computer and cell phone for twenty-four hours; the e-mail and voice mail can wait.

24. Take a walk; if you see flowers, stop and smell them.

25. Take a nap in the middle of the day on your day of rest.

26. Join your spiritual community at your place of worship on the day of rest.

27. Make sure your family and friends are getting rest— and if they're not, offer them respite so they can take some time off.

28. Invite family and friends to share a Sabbath meal.

29. Pray, sing, study, snuggle—for a whole day!

30. Plan a vacation. Take it. Leave your laptop at home.

4
Call

God likes to call human beings.

Not phone calls.

God calls.

God is calling all the time.

People call God all the time, too.

These calls are called prayer.

In the Bible, God hears and answers calls.

If God makes and answers calls, shouldn't you?

The first of God's calls in the Bible is to Adam and Eve, human beings made in the divine image to be God's partners.

Here's the scene (Gen. 2:15–3:8):

God had made Adam and placed him in the Garden of Eden, telling him to eat the fruit of any tree, except the Tree of Knowledge of Good and Evil. Then, God decides it is not good for man to be alone. So, God fashions a woman, Eve, who has not heard the warning directly from God, but nevertheless knows about the prohibition when confronted by the serpent, who deviously suggests she could eat from the tree. She eats the fruit from the Tree of Knowledge of Good and Evil, and her husband eats. Their eyes are opened, and they perceive their nakedness and slink into the Garden when they hear the "sound of the Lord God moving about the Garden in the breezy time of day."

God calls.

In fact, God asks the very first *question* in the Bible:

"*Ayekah?*—Where are you?" (Gen. 3:9).

This question is not simply a query of location. This is an existential question.

God is asking about the relationship of Adam to his Maker. God had told him not to do something, but Adam did it anyway. This was a violation of their relationship.

Between the lines of the text, I hear a deeply disappointed God saying: "I gave you permission to eat anything, anything at all in this fantastic garden, except the fruit from one tree. One tree!?! And, you go ahead and eat of it! I'm calling you on this.... "

And God did call him on it. God calls all three of them on it—the man, the woman, and the serpent. God condemns the serpent to crawl on its belly and eat dirt. God makes childbearing pangs severe for the woman and tilling the soil backbreaking work for the man. Ultimately, God throws all of them out of the Garden of Eden.

Where are you?

Where are you in your relationship with God?

Are you listening when God calls?

Can you hear the still, small voice of conscience that asks you to do the right thing?

Will you respond to God's call to be God's partner?

Responding to the Call

If Adam and Eve heard God's call to accountability, Abraham heard the call to take the journey.

Imagine if Abraham lived in a time when there was a phone.

It rings.

Abram (his biblical name at the time, later changed to Abraham) picks up the phone. The deep voice on the other end says (Gen. 12:1):

"Go."

In my imagination, Abram replies: "What?"

"Go," the voice repeats, "out from your native land and from your father's house ... "

"Oh, really?" Abram might have thought as he heard this strange voice. "And where should I *go* to?"

" … to a land that I will show you," God continues.

In the biblical account, of course, Abram says nothing. He is silent. Perhaps God knew that this call would be difficult for Abram to accept. So, God adds an incentive for Abram to take the journey.

I will make of you a great nation,
And I will bless you;
I will make your name great,
And you shall be a blessing.
I will bless those that bless you
And curse him that curses you;
And all the families of the earth
Shall bless themselves by you.

GENESIS 12:2–3

Wow! Fortune, fame, blessing, protection, and power await him if Abram accepts the call.

In the next few verses of the chapter, we discover that Abram was a wealthy man, seventy-five years old at the time of God's call. He was married and had a close extended family. Yet, this man, who will in time come to challenge and argue with God, listens to the divine summons and responds without as much as a whisper of protest. The Bible records Abram's response to the call: "Abram went out as the Lord had commanded him.… " (Gen. 12:4).

What is God calling you to do?

What is God calling you to do?

My mother, Bernice, heard God's call to work for the blind children of the state of Nebraska in the 1950s. A friend, Pauline Guss, had told her about witnessing a young blind man, Sparky Mandel, thank a local congregational sisterhood for help in transcribing a Braille prayer book so he could have a bar mitzvah. She asked Bernice to investigate whether it would be possible to start a Braille group in the synagogue. In short order it was done, and Mom and her friends published the first English-Hebrew Passover Haggadah in Braille.

One thing quickly led to another. Mom learned that there were eight blind kids in Omaha who needed a preschool, but no institution would host them. She knew that the synagogue preschool met on Monday, Wednesday, and Friday mornings, so she asked her rabbi, Myer S. Kripke, whether the blind kids could come on Tuesday and Thursday. Done. She then thought the kids would benefit from a summer camp experience. She took Gene Eppley, the richest man in Omaha at the time (Eppley Air Field is named for him), out to the Salvation Army camp, where one of the talented blind kids entertained. The next day, Eppley called to offer $10,000, but it had to be given to a 501c3 nonprofit corporation. Overnight, Mom established the Nebraska Foundation for Visually Impaired Children to gather funding and support. She thought the kids should have an annual Christmas party; the blind children got $25 each and a helper to go shopping for Christmas presents for their parents and siblings.

One of the proudest days of my life was when this busy mom, with three little kids of her own, was honored as the Omaha "Volunteer of the Year" in 1961. I even got to leave school early to attend the luncheon! To this day, the Foundation and the Braille group continue their important work in improving the lives of the blind children and adults in Nebraska.

Making Calls

Speaking of mothers, have you talked to yours lately?

Look at this commandment, number five on God's Original Top Ten To-Do List:

"Honor your father and mother...."

EXODUS 20:12

Notice the commandment is not "*Love* Your Father and Mother." You would think that is what God would have put on the To-Do List, no?

God is smarter than that.

Some children end up not loving their parents. But God still wants children to *honor* them.

What does it mean to honor parents? What can be put on God's To-Do List that would reflect the meaning of this instruction?

Honoring someone requires, at the very minimum, recognizing his or her existence.

So, how about adding this to God's To-Do List:

Call your mother!

Stuart Matlins tells a wonderful story about a man hearing the call of his wife. The couple had a very close and loving relationship, but as is evident in this particular incident, it was often the wife who called on the husband to respond. One early evening, as the husband was heading from the living room toward the bedroom, his wife called out to him: "Put on a sweater." The husband replied: "Are we going out—or am I cold?"

In an age when many people communicate electronically via e-mail, we are in danger of losing the power of the personal call.

Harvey Bodansky is a sixty-year-old man who has lived with severe cerebral palsy since he was a child. Brilliant and funny, Harvey is a leading advocate for people with special needs who want to achieve a college education. Although his speech is extremely labored, Harvey communicates well. We met when his father, Harry, brought Harvey to a convention where I was speaking, and we became fast friends.

Every year, on our respective birthdays, I call Harvey and Harvey calls me. We catch up on our lives, our work, our families. Harvey has an echoic memory; he unfailingly remembers everything I have told him over the years. To know another human being who daily overcomes enormous obstacles and yet makes significant contributions to making the world a better place is a great gift. I put Harvey's birthday on my calendar so I won't forget to call. It's a good idea to put all of your loved ones' birthdays on your calendar so you won't forget to call. Receiving a call on your birthday is one of the simplest yet most appreciated reminders that you are loved.

Isadore Bogdanoff understood the importance of making calls. A retired clothier, he was a regular at his local community center and congregation, making many friends. Once you became a friend of "Boggy" (as he was fondly known), you made it to his "call-list." Every day, Boggy would make phone calls to his friends, checking in on them to see if they were okay or needed anything. He especially looked after elderly friends who lived alone, realizing that one of their most important needs was to know that someone cared. When he died, hundreds of Boggy's call-list friends came to the funeral, celebrating this extraordinary man, knowing how much they would miss his calls of caring.

Resisting the Temptation to Resist the Call

It's not always easy to hear God's call. It's even tougher to act on it.

Take Moses, for example.

Here's a guy of privilege, raised in the palace of Egypt by Pharaoh, the Egyptian ruler, unaware that his real identity is that of an Israelite. But when he sees a Hebrew slave being beaten by an Egyptian taskmaster, something in him is kindled to protect the man, and he kills the Egyptian. Knowing that he has just committed an act that will forever cut him off from the aristocracy that raised him, he flees to the land of Midian. There, he marries a Midianite woman, has two sons—one he names "stranger"—and settles into life as a shepherd.

Meanwhile, back in Egypt, the suffering of the Israelites increased:

> *The Israelites were groaning under the bondage and cried out; and their cry for help from the bondage rose up to God. God heard their moaning, and God remembered His covenant with Abraham and Isaac and Jacob. God looked upon the Israelites, and God took notice of them.*
> EXODUS 2:23–25

God hears calls, too, and responds.

God calls Moses to leadership (Exodus 3 and 4). While tending his flock, Moses sees a bush all aflame, yet, according to the Bible, "the bush was not consumed" (Exo. 3:2). Moses says: "I must turn aside to look at this marvelous sight; why doesn't the bush burn up?" When God sees that he has noticed, "God called to him out of the bush: Moses! Moses!"

How did Moses respond to the direct divine call?

At first, Moses responds with a spontaneous, unhesitating answer: "*Hineini*—Here I am!"

(From a close reading of the Bible, "Here I am" is clearly the appropriate response when God calls. In fact, the Hebrew term appears fourteen times in the Bible. For example, when Abraham is about to sacrifice his favorite child, Isaac, an angel of God calls to him, "Abraham! Abraham!" and Abraham answers: "*Hineini*—Here I am" [Gen. 22:11].)

After God explains the call—I am coming to rescue my covenanted people from the bonds of slavery, and you, my boy, are to be my personal representative to Pharaoh to demand their freedom—Moses questions the call: "Who am I that I should go to Pharaoh and free the Israelites from Egypt?"

Although God reassures him that "I will be with you," Moses has a second objection:

"When I come to the Israelites and say to them, 'The God of your fathers has sent me to you,' and they ask me, 'What is His name?' what shall I say to them?"

God then reveals the divine name, "*Ehyeh-asher-Ehyeh*—I Will Be What I Will Be," and gives precise instructions to Moses.

For a third time, Moses objects:

"But Moses spoke up and said, 'What if they do not believe me and do not listen to me, but say: The Lord did not appear to you?'"

> When your family, friends, and community call on you, will you answer: "Here I am"?

So God shows Moses the power of divine intervention through a series of transformations that will upstage the magicians of Egypt.

Nevertheless, Moses objects a fourth and final time:

"But, Moses said to the Lord, 'Please, O Lord, I have never been a man of words, either in times past or now that You have spoken to Your servant; I am slow of speech and slow of tongue.... Please, O Lord, make someone else Your agent.'"

At this point, God gets angry with Moses and calls on Aaron, Moses' brother, to be his spokesman; together, the two brothers will confront Pharaoh.

The biblical story recognizes how hard it is to hear God's call and respond.

In fact, the most famous of all Jewish prayers, the Shema, begins with the word *hear*:

"Hear, O Israel, the Lord our God, the Lord is One."

Your purpose in life is to serve God, to be God's messenger, to do God's work.

When God calls, will you hear and answer: *"Hineini"*?

When your family, friends, and community call on you, will you answer: "Here I am"?

God's To-Do List

 Call

31. Call your parents, spouse, children, siblings, aunts and uncles, cousins, and friends—just to check in.

32. Practice hearing. Listen to a loved one or a colleague speak, and don't interrupt.

33. Return messages and e-mails from others as soon as possible. They are calling you.

34. Respect all questions from others, and give them an answer.

35. Answer this question regularly: Where am I?

36. Call your congressperson about a cause you believe in. Call the president to share how you feel about an issue—(202) 456-1111 (comments) or (202) 456-1414 (switchboard).

37. Call on your friends to join you in volunteering.

38. Study how biblical figures answer God's call.

39. Listen for God's call. You'll know it when you hear it.

40. Respond to God's call. Remember, you are on a mission from God to do God's work on earth.

_____

_____

_____

_____

Comfort

In the Bible, God makes house calls.

Not too often, mind you.

But, when God decides to visit, you can bet something important is about to happen.

Here is the story of one such divine visit to Abraham:

> *The Lord appeared to him by the terebinths of Mamre; he (Abraham) was sitting at the entrance of the tent as the day grew hot. Looking up, he saw three men standing near him. As soon as he saw them, he ran from the entrance of the tent to greet them and, bowing to the ground, he said, "My lords, if it please you, do not go on past your servant. Let a little water be brought; bathe your feet and recline under the tree. And let me fetch a morsel of bread that you may refresh yourselves; then go on—seeing that you have come your servant's way." They replied, "Do as you have said."*
>
> GENESIS 18:1–5

The biblical commentators have a field day with this story. They begin by asking: What was Abraham doing as he sat in the heat of the day at the entrance of his tent? The medieval commentator Rashi points out that he was healing; after all, as noted earlier, Abraham had just circumcised him-self at the age of ninety-nine! The very next line of the Bible says that "the Lord appeared to him"; in other words, God was visiting the sick to offer comfort to Abraham. And yet, when the three strangers come into view, Abraham overcomes his pain, interrupts his visit with God, and rushes to greet them, to be hospitable and offer them comfort and respite from their journey.

Visiting the Sick

Have you ever been sick? *Really* sick? In the hospital sick?

It's awful. You feel terrible. You are alone and isolated from your family and friends. Your mind races with thoughts of your own mortality. You need comfort, reassurance, support.

When you visit someone who is sick, you are God's messenger.

You are bringing encouragement, connection, hope. You are caring for the ill by sharing your love.

> When you visit someone who is sick, you are God's messenger.

Every week, Judy Bin-Nun and her dogs Zeesee, Ketzel, and Raizel visit sick people in hospitals. The dogs, three adorable Brussels griffon (they look like Ewoks from *Star Wars*), have been specially trained for this work. They jump into the laps of bedridden patients, who immediately perk up and smile as they pet and brush the animals. Judy—and her dogs—are doing God's work.

It was the car accident that began the irrevocable decline of Joe Rothkop's health. With a severely broken leg, Joe endured a long recuperation period at a rehabilitation facility. It was there that he met Boysie Sarmiento, a young nurse assistant working in the physical therapy clinic. The two of them hit it off instantly, and their story is one of caring and healing, giving and receiving, living and learning—and love.

You couldn't find two more seemingly dissimilar people. Joe, a tall, handsome, nearly ninety-year-old man who hailed from the Midwest, and Boysie, a diminutive, wispy, twenty-year-old immigrant from the Philippines, were brought together through the need for healing: patient and caregiver. In the often stifling atmosphere of the rehab center, caring for stroke victims and mangled bodies is a challenging and frustrating job. But Joe, his wife Harriet, and their two daughters, Michele and Sonja, noticed that Boysie never seemed to let it all get to him. If he was embarrassed or sickened by the tasks he was asked to do, Boysie never let on. He approached each day, each interaction, with a smile and an attitude that came from some deep reservoir of caring for another human being. Joe responded to this, himself a person of great warmth and welcome.

When Joe was finally ready to return to his home, the family asked Boysie whether he was interested in becoming Joe's full-time caregiver. Boysie had only recently graduated a program to become a nurse assistant and had never taken on that kind of responsibility. But he had a fondness for Joe that developed over the months of his rehabilitation. So, he agreed.

Most of the time, they would giggle. Two men giggling—over inside jokes, funny situations, and Joe's attempts at humor. Joe loved a good story, and he told them over and over again. Boysie laughed and laughed, no matter how many times he heard them. As Boysie's English steadily improved, Joe would sometimes ask Boysie to tell these stories himself.

Boysie's English wasn't the only language that was improving. Joe set about teaching Hebrew and Yiddish to Boysie. Joe was not very religious, but he loved being Jewish. One day, while Boysie was pushing Joe in his wheelchair out the front door, Joe noticed a five-pound box of matzah on the hallway table. "What's that?" Joe asked Boysie. "Oh, that's our matzahs, Joe," Boysie matter-of-factly responded.

The affection between Joe and Boysie was palpable. Joe was like a father to him, encouraging his studies and his dreams. More than anything, Boysie wanted to become an American citizen. Joe was back at a rehab center when Boysie passed his exam and got his papers. When Boysie returned from the court that day, Joe and the family arranged a huge party to celebrate his accomplishment, complete with Uncle Sam hats for the nurses, Sousa marching music, and an enormous cake.

Harriet recalls that no matter how difficult it was to take care of Joe, Boysie always had a smile and a warm word. He not only cared for Joe's physical condition, but he also listened and learned as Joe taught him life lessons, enabling Joe to be a teacher, a mentor, and a guide. In a way, both of them were giving care to each other.

As the end came, Joe was surrounded by his family, his friends, and Boysie. Each of us was privileged to say our good-bye to Joe, to hold his hand, to kiss his forehead, to let him go. When it was Boysie's turn, he caressed Joe's face, tears in his eyes, and said simply: "*Gei shlofen* [go to sleep], Joe."

At the funeral, warm expressions of love were extended by Harriet, Sonja and her husband Dave, and Michele to all of the people who knew Joe. But perhaps the most heartfelt thanks were offered to Boysie, for giving care, dignity, laughter, and love to their beloved husband and father.

Comforting the Sick

There is no end to the gratitude we have for those unusual human beings who are the true healers in our midst.

There is an art to offering comfort to the sick and the elderly. The most important thing is to be there. Go to the hospital, the home, the house, the hospice. Bring something to cheer up the patient—flowers, balloons, magazines, books, cards. These things left behind after you leave are a continuation of your presence. Position yourself at the level of the patient; don't stand over the bed. Invite the person to talk about his experience, but don't be surprised if he would rather not. Tell him stories, jokes, and news of family, friends, and the world. Ask whether there is anything special you can do for the person—drive a carpool, make a phone call, or get groceries for the family at home.

Bring photos. Play favorite music. Watch a television program together. Read aloud a book or newspaper. Hold hands. Wash her face with a cold cloth. Massage her back or feet. Provide ice chips or fresh drinking water.

Don't stay too long on your visit. Sick people get exhausted quickly. Before you leave, if you believe the gesture will be appreciated, ask permission to offer a blessing of healing. If you don't know a formal blessing, "God bless you and heal you" works just fine.

Consoling the Mourner

Have you ever been at a funeral or walked into a house of mourning and not known what to say? I know many people who avoid going to funerals or visiting with mourners because they are afraid they'll say something wrong. Often, they do:

"She lived a long life."

"There, there—get ahold of yourself."

"I know exactly what you're going through."

"You'll get pregnant again."

"It's probably for the best."

The truth is: you don't have to say anything. Just be there. Offer a hand, a hug, an arm around the shoulder. If you must say something, say, "I'm sorry for your loss." When the mourner wants to talk, encourage the person to share memories of the loved one who died. The most comforting thing you can do is show up—even if it is difficult for you.

Welcoming the Stranger

Let's revisit the biblical account of Abraham's tent. When you read the text this time, notice the verbs. They are the clue to the true meaning of the story.

> The Lord appeared to him by the terebinths of Mamre; he (Abraham) was sitting at the entrance of the tent as the day grew hot. Looking up, he saw three men standing near him. As soon as he saw them, he ran from the entrance of the tent to greet them and, bowing to the ground, he said, "My lords, if it please you, do not go on past your servant. Let a little water be brought; bathe your feet and recline under the tree. And let me fetch a morsel of bread that you may refresh yourselves; then go on—seeing that you have come your servant's way." They replied, "Do as you have said." Abraham hastened into the tent to Sarah, and said, "Quick, three seahs of choice flour! Knead and make cakes!" Then Abraham ran to the herd, took a calf, tender and choice, and gave it to a servant-boy, who hastened to prepare it. He took curds and milk and the calf that had been prepared and set these before them; and he waited on them under the tree as they ate.
>
> GENESIS 18:1–8

This is a text in a hurry. Look at the words used to describe Abraham's actions: he ran, he rushed, he hastened, "Quick!" The Hebrew verbs are even more dramatic: *vayaratz, vayimaheir, mahari!* The word for *run* is used twice, *rushed* three times, and *fetch* four times. To Abraham, the three strangers were sojourners in need of comfort and respite, and he implored them to enjoy the hospitality of his and Sarah's tent. From this example, the Talmud teaches this remarkable lesson: "Welcoming strangers is more important than welcoming God's presence" (*Shabbat* 127a). After all, God was visiting the sick, and yet, Abraham ran to greet his guests.

> There is an imperative even greater than talking with God; be like God.

Can you imagine yourself being visited by a great political figure, or a famous celebrity, and three strangers walk by, and you say, "Excuse me. I'll be right back," and run out to greet them?

That's what the story is all about.

There is an imperative even greater than talking with God; *be like God.*

Visit, offer comfort, extend hospitality to make anyone feel at home.

There is an even more remarkable lesson in this story. Abraham knows nothing at all about the strangers. They could have been beggars off the street or wealthy big shots. It didn't matter to Abraham.

He practiced what might be called the *spirituality of welcoming.*

It is a practice high up on God's To-Do List.

The spirituality of welcoming elevates both the guest and the host. For the guest, a warm greeting sets one at ease by relieving the unspoken anxiety of the stranger and immediately answering the first question anyone in a strange place asks: "Will I be welcome here?" For the host, the act of hospitality is a gesture of spiritual generosity, uplifting the soul. It is an offering of oneself, an invitation for connection—between human and human, and in that meeting, between human and God.

In our first year of marriage, Susie and I took a trip to Israel and stopped in Rome on the way. On the long flight from St. Louis to Italy, we sat next to a nice young man, who began chatting with us. Nick was a college student, traveling to Rome to meet up with his recent Italian bride, Daniela, who had gone ahead to help her family prepare for the Christmas holiday. After talking for what seemed like hours about life as newlyweds, he asked where we were staying in Rome, and we told him the name of our hotel. As we landed, we wished each other well on our journeys, thinking we would never see him again.

The next day, we received a completely unexpected phone call. It was Nick. "I told Daniela and her family about you. Would you like to come over to the house for a meal tomorrow night?" We accepted this gesture of hospitality immediately.

As I gave the directions to a cab driver, I suddenly turned to Susie and said: "We barely know this guy. What are we doing? Where are we going?" The cab driver let us off at the designated address, in front of a stately building, directly across from the Tiber River, in what was clearly an upscale neighborhood. We entered the lobby and found the name of the family—Bini—on a buzzer. Nick answered: "Welcome! We've been expecting you. Take the elevator."

There was only one apartment on the penthouse floor, and it belonged to Mr. and Mrs. Bini. We were met with hugs and kisses on both cheeks by Daniela, Nick's gorgeous wife, who greeted us like long-lost friends. The senior Binis spoke broken English, but somehow we communicated well. Daniela had learned from Nick that we followed the laws of keeping kosher, she told the family, and they arranged to have a vegetarian entrée during the phenomenal feast. After the after-dinner drinks, Nick and Daniela took us on a drive to see the Seven Hills of Rome and several piazzas, beautifully decorated for the holiday. For a couple of Jewish kids, it was a wonderful Christmas! And a remarkable act of hospitality and welcoming of strangers that we will never forget.

Radical Hospitality

There is a deeper meaning to the practice of visiting, offering comfort, and welcoming. Call it radical hospitality. It is a hospitality borne of a core value that is the basis of all of the actions on God's To-Do List:

Every human being is made in the image of God.

Every human being is made in the image of God.

Be present.

Be God's agent on earth.

When you visit, you bring God's presence to those who need it most.

When you offer comfort, you are doing God's work.

When you welcome the stranger, you are welcoming God's angels in the world.

God's To-Do List

 ## Comfort

41. When your friends or relatives are sick, bring them soup, ginger ale, tea, tissues.

42. When you visit people in the hospital, bring them something to read, a funny story, their favorite music, photos of their loved ones.

43. Let someone go in front of you in line; yield to someone trying to merge into traffic.

44. Make a donation, say a blessing, offer your prayers to God for healing.

45. When you see someone who looks sad or unwell, ask whether there's anything you can do to help.

46. Go to funerals; comfort the mourner at the wake or shiva with your presence.

47. Put a "Welcome" sign at the entrance to your home.

48. Invite newcomers in your neighborhood to your home for a meal.

49. Take new colleagues in your company out to lunch.

50. Visit a senior center or retirement community.

_____

_____

_____

_____

6
Care

Caring for another is a lost art. It seems that only when there is a tragedy—September 11th, Hurricane Katrina, massive earthquakes—do people find the kindness that is often hidden in their souls.

The Bible is replete with references to the caring and kindness (*hesed* is the Hebrew term) of God.

Just before Jacob's encounter with Esau, he thanks God:

> *O God of my father Abraham and God of my father Isaac, O Lord, who said to me, "Return to your native land and I will deal bountifully with you!" I am unworthy of all the kindness* (hahasadim) *that You have so steadfastly shown Your servant.*
>
> GENESIS 32:10–11

When Joseph is thrown into jail in Egypt, we are told:

> *The Lord was with Joseph: He extended kindness* (hesed) *to him and disposed the chief jailer favorably toward him.*
>
> GENESIS 39:21

When the People Israel learn that the Promised Land of Canaan was fortified with vast armies, they complain to Moses that the forty years in the desert has led them to the eve of destruction. God once again threatens to annihilate them for not trusting divine power, and Moses begs for patience:

> *Therefore, I pray, let my Lord's forbearance be great, as You have declared, saying, "The Lord! slow to anger and abounding in kindness* (hesed); *forgiving iniquity and transgression" … Pardon, I pray, the*

iniquity of this people according to Your great kindness (hasdekha), as You have forgiven this people ever since Egypt.

NUMBERS 14:17–19

In the Talmud, Rabbi Elazar quotes a famous verse from the prophet Micah:

You have been told what is good and what the Lord requires of you: to act justly, to love kindness (hesed), and to walk humbly with your God.

MICAH 6:8

Rabbi Elazar then asks: "What does this verse imply?" "To act justly" means to act in accordance with the principles of justice. "To love kindness" means to let your actions be guided by principles of lovingkindness (Hebrew: *gemillut hasadim*). "To walk humbly with your God" means to assist needy families at their funerals and weddings by giving humbly, in private.

Here is another text on the meaning of lovingkindness:

Our rabbis taught: Acts of lovingkindness are superior to charity in three respects. Charity can be accomplished only through money; acts of lovingkindness can be accomplished through personal involvement as well as with money. Charity can be given only to the poor; acts of lovingkindness can be done for both the rich and the poor. Charity applies only to the living; acts of lovingkindness apply to both the living and the dead.

> The ultimate kindness is to save a life.

Rabbi Elazar said: Whoever does acts of charity and justice is considered as having filled the world with lovingkindness, as it is written, "He loves charity and justice; the earth is filled with the lovingkindness (hesed) of the Lord (Psalm 33:5)."

SUKKAH 49B

What is an act of lovingkindness?

Save a Life—Save a World

The ultimate kindness is to save a life.

A remarkable saying from the Jewish tradition is this:

> *Whoever destroys a soul, it is considered as if the person destroyed an*
> *entire world. And whoever saves a life, it is considered as if the person*
> *saved an entire world.*

JERUSALEM TALMUD, SANHEDRIN 4:1

Ira's parents went to visit him while he was attending Columbia University in the early 1970s, a time when New York City was not exactly the safest place on earth, especially for tourists who did not know the ways of the city. On the second day of their visit, Ira was rushed to the hospital and had an emergency appendectomy. Uncertain about how to get from midtown to the hospital and completely disoriented by the canyons of tall buildings, his parents stood on the street in front of their hotel, waiting for an uptown bus. A man standing at the bus stop said to them: "Do you have the exact change for the bus?" Ira's father was twenty-five cents short. The stranger gave him a quarter.

The bus arrived; Ira's parents got on and asked the driver, "Will this take us to St. Luke's Hospital?" The driver took a look at them and said, "Yes." He drove one block, then suddenly called Ira's father to the front of the bus. "Listen," the driver said emphatically, handing him a transfer slip, "you don't want this bus. Get off here and walk one block west to Broadway. Get on the bus going uptown. Go!" They got off, found the other bus, and made their way to Ira's hospital room. When they walked in, two of Ira's friends were there visiting him. After telling the story, Ira's mother asked: "Why in the world did that bus driver tell us to get off his bus?" One of the guys said: "Whew, you are pretty darn lucky he did. If you had stayed on that bus, you would have had to walk through Morningside Heights Park to get here. Gangs hang out there looking for anyone they think they can mug. Last week, a man was killed walking through that park. That bus driver knew you would have been in grave danger. He probably saved your life."

Joanie Rosen saved a life.

Her brother's life.

Joanie is darling, caring, and quick with a word of praise and encouragement. She has pet names for everyone in her family—a niece is "Rebecca of Sunnybrook Farm," newlyweds are "Ken and Barbie," a young cousin is *"gute, gute, gute"* ("good" in Yiddish). Joanie's home is decorated in everything red, white, and blue, like something out of the *Martha Stewart Living* Fourth of July issue. She is just plain fun to be around.

One day, Joanie got one of those calls that everyone fears, and only a few answer.

Her brother Gary, in Chicago, who had been suffering from kidney disease, was in danger of dying if a donor was not found.

Joanie immediately volunteered to be tested to see whether she could be a match, and the test came back positive.

Joanie was elated; she wanted to give her brother the gift of life. Their father had died of renal failure at the age of sixty-two—her brother was forty. He always said he wanted to try to stay healthy and live longer. But here he was, in danger of dying, needing the kidney that his sister was stepping up to give.

Gary didn't want her to do it, to risk her life to save his. "Pony," he said—he called her Pony because she always wore a ponytail as a little girl—"Pony, it's too dangerous."

But Joanie would have none of that.

The surgery was scheduled at a hospital in Wisconsin. Both Joanie and Gary were prepped for surgery simultaneously. There they were, sedated, lying on gurneys, brother and sister, side by side. As Joanie tells the story, Gary was already nearly under, but she was not. She got up from the gurney, walked over to Gary, took his hand, and whispered, "Gary, now you'll have the quality of life you deserve." Although Joanie thought her brother was out for the count, he squeezed her hand as if to say thank you.

The surgery was a complete success. Gary recovered and did get the quality of life he had not had for years. Joanie also recovered—although it took quite a while longer than expected—and to this day, she lives with one kidney.

Joanie resumed her life with her husband, Paul, and their two boys, with all the ups and downs twenty years of living will bring.

And then one day, Paul came home from work with skin the shade of pale yellow. Within six months, the cancer had engulfed him, and he died at the age of fifty-five. Joanie was devastated, but she refused to be defeated. She held herself up through this tragic loss, caring for her two boys, a daughter-in-law, and a new grandchild.

Then, after more than twenty years of good health due to her donated kidney, Gary suddenly fell into a coma. She rushed to Chicago to his bedside in a hospice. He had not awakened in two days. Undeterred, Joanie took his hand in hers and said: "Gary, I love you." He opened his eyes and said, "I love you, Pony ... " He died the next day.

John, her oldest son, said to Joanie: "Mom, so many terrible things have happened to our family, I don't know if I believe in God anymore."

Joanie said to her son: "John, you have to believe. You have to have hope. If you have no hope, you have nothing. I have hope. I have hope that tomorrow will be better than yesterday. Maybe it will be; maybe it won't. But I have to believe that it will be a better day tomorrow."

Joanie gave gifts of lovingkindness—the gift of life to her brother and the gift of hope to her son.

Why is one life so important? Can one life make a difference in the world?

When the Israelites were fleeing Pharaoh's army and found themselves facing the Reed Sea, God told Moses, "Command the Israelites to move forward. Hold your staff over the Sea, and it will split, and you will cross in safety." But the people were afraid. They thought they would drown.

One person, Nachshon ben Aminadav, had the courage and faith to step into the water, to take action. He waded out farther and farther, until the water came up to his nostrils and he could no longer breathe. Only then did the sea split.

Nachshon cared about his family and his people, and he took the first step—literally—to demonstrate how much he cared.

One life is all it takes to affect the world.

Making a Difference

Everyone wants to matter.

Everyone wants to make a difference.

You can.

Every day.

With simple acts of caring and kindness.

A wonderful story about caring was popularized in the first *Chicken Soup for the Soul* book, but like many stories that enter the imagination of the people, its origins are not well known. It is based on an essay by a scientist and poet, Loren Eiseley, who included it in a book of his writings entitled *The Unexpected Universe*. Today, there are literally hundreds of versions of the story on the Internet and it is heard regularly in graduation speeches and inspirational seminars. Why? Because it illustrates a deep truth: every act you do matters to someone or something in God's universe.

> Everyone wants to make a difference.

The gist of the story is simple: a man walking along a beach meets someone picking up stranded starfish and throwing them back in the ocean, saving them from certain death. There are hundreds of starfish strewn on the sand. The observer comments that the star thrower's efforts seem futile; he cannot possible make a difference. As the star thrower tosses another live starfish into the sea, he says: "Made a difference to that one."

Show You Care

God performs acts of lovingkindness. The Bible is filled with the stories of how God cares. In Jewish tradition, the morning prayers include these words from the Bible:

> *You shall be holy, for I, the Lord your God, am holy.... You shall not insult the deaf, or put a stumbling block before the blind. You shall not render an unjust decision; do not be partial to the poor or show deference to the rich: judge your neighbor fairly. Do not stand idly by the blood of your*

neighbor. You shall not hate your brother in your heart. Love your neighbor as yourself; I am the Lord.

LEVITICUS *19:2, 14–18*

You can care, too. By doing acts of goodness every day. By making a difference to just one person.

Who knows?

Perhaps you can do something today that the world—your world—may talk about for years to come.

God's To-Do List

 Care

51. Make a difference in someone's life today by simply caring: hold a door for a stranger; hug a loved one.

52. Perform a random act of kindness—on purpose.

53. Go to Oprah Winfrey's website, www.oprah.com, click on "Oprah's Angel Network," follow the links to the "Kindness Chain" and be inspired to begin one.

54. While you're on the Internet, send a greeting card to a friend, just to brighten his or her day. Try www.bluemountain.com or Hallmark E-Cards at www.hallmark.com.

55. Leave flowers on the front door of a neighbor— without a card.

56. Bring coffee and a treat—cookies, bagels, cake—to the office.

57. Take a resident of an elder-care facility for a ride in the car.

58. Remind your children to call their grandparents on their birthdays.

59. Never part from your loved ones without kissing them good-bye, no matter what.

60. Always say "I love you" at the end of phone calls with loved ones and friends. You never know whether it will be your last opportunity to tell them.

_____

_____

_____

Repair

God created the world, but it is not perfect. Not by any means.

Children go to bed hungry.

Vicious people commit acts of genocide.

Nations lift up swords against nations.

The homeless sleep on the streets.

The world needs repair people.

In Jewish tradition, at the climax of the prayer service recited three times a day that recognizes the Oneness of God, the liturgy reads:

> [You are] to repair the world for the sake of bringing God's Reign on earth, so that all humankind will call Your Name....

This is the call to social justice. This is the recognition that God left work to be done to perfect the world, to repair its brokenness—*tikkun olam*—to strive for *shalom,* a Hebrew term normally translated as "peace," but that comes from the root word for "wholeness."

You cannot be whole when the world is not whole.

The spark of divinity in you is moved when you encounter a human being, made in the image of God, in desperate need. This is not just about generosity of spirit; it is about the Spirit Within calling the heart to act.

The Bible is replete with laws that reflect a deep concern for the disadvantaged, the stranger, the widow, and the orphan. God says:

The world needs repair people.

*You shall not wrong a stranger, or oppress him, for you were strangers in
the land of Egypt. You shall not ill-treat any widow or orphan. If you do
mistreat them, I will heed their outcry as soon as they cry out to Me....*

*If you lend money to My people, to the poor among you, do not act
toward them as a creditor; exact no interest from them. If you take your
neighbor's garment in pledge, you must return it to him before the sun sets; it
is his only clothing, the sole covering for his skin. In what else shall he sleep?
Therefore, if he cries out to Me, I will pay heed, for I am compassionate.*

EXODUS 22:20–26

How will you repair the world?

Repair People

Danny Siegel devotes his time and energy to repairing the world. More
than thirty years ago, he created a nonprofit fund to assist what he calls
"Mitzvah heroes." (*Mitzvah* is the Hebrew term for "To-Do," often translated as "commandment"; in this context, it means "good deed.") He
searches the world for individuals who have dedicated their lives to serving others, people like:

- Ranya Kelly, the shoe lady of Denver, who began her work
  when she found five hundred pairs of brand-new shoes in a
  Dumpster. Today, twenty years later, she has salvaged more than
  $23 million in usable items to distribute to people in need.

- PK Beville, who founded Second Wind Dreams to make the
  dreams of elders come true.

- John Beltzer, who created Songs of Love, a group of musicians
  who compose original songs for children with life-threatening
  medical conditions.

- Jeannie Jaybush, who meets the needs of new moms and their
  babies at St. Joseph's Baby Corner in Seattle.

- Clara Hammer, the Chicken Lady of Jerusalem, who was so out-
  raged at the sight of a poor woman who begged a butcher for
  bones to make soup that she established a Chicken Fund
  twenty-two years ago that today enables more than two

hundred fifty needy families to have a chicken for their Sabbath dinner every week. She was seventy-two years old when she started her repair work.

Danny himself is an indefatigable teacher and advocate of fixing the world. He draws inspiration from his prodigious knowledge of Jewish values and examples such as the Giraffe Heroes Project, which celebrates those who "stick their necks out" to make the world a better place. When he began his Ziv Tzedakah Fund in 1975, he raised $955, which he distributed to unknown mitzvah heroes. In 2005 alone, Danny collected and distributed nearly $2 million to dozens of projects led by extraordinary people of all religions, races, and creeds. Reading his annual report, filled with moving stories of the holy work these heroes do, is a most inspiring experience; see www.ziv.org.

David Levinson is a screenwriter. He belongs to a wonderful congregation, Temple Israel of Hollywood. Inspired to do something good for the community, he compiled a list of small tasks that could be done in a day—painting, landscaping, fix-it work—for a variety of groups in neighborhoods across Los Angeles. On a Sunday in 1999, he recruited three hundred of his fellow congregants to join him in doing a mitzvah. Those who participated not only had a great time doing the work, but they also felt useful, needed, elevated. The next year, six hundred people volunteered for the Mitzvah Day. The social service groups that benefited from the one-day avalanche of help began to talk about it, and the word-of-mouth spread through the city. Churches asked to participate, and the number of schools, clubs, and agencies needing help mushroomed. By 2002, the project was attracting fifteen hundred people who wanted to donate a day of their time to repairing the world.

As more people stepped forward to get involved, Levinson and Temple Israel's board of trustees changed the name of the project to Big Sunday. Big Sunday has evolved into a huge undertaking, with more than thirty thousand people, from all walks of life, working together on projects as diverse as cooking meals to installing sprinkler systems. Teenagers put on shows for senior citizens, and volunteers plant gardens

and clean beaches. Congregants from dozens of churches and synagogues put on pancake breakfasts and prepare food baskets for the
homeless. Even the mayor of Los Angeles, Antonio Villaraigosa, lent his
support, partnering his Citywide Day of Service with Big Sunday. A
small repair project turned with a major community-building event.

The motto for Big Sunday says it all:

No matter who you are, no matter where you live, no matter what you do,
everyone has some way they can help someone else.

Of course, Levinson and his colleagues understand that devoting one day
of volunteering will hardly repair the world, but it's a start. And by
recruiting so many people in the city of angels to taste the joy and the
fulfillment of serving others and fixing that which is broken, the hope is
that the one day will turn into a lifetime of service, giving them a new
understanding of the importance of doing God's work on earth. See
www.bigsunday.org for more inspiration.

God creates human beings with the instruction to "be fertile and
increase, fill the earth and master it.... " In Los Angeles, as in many
cities throughout the world, this has led to overpopulation, industrial-
ization, and the poisoning of the environment.

When Andy Lipkis was a fifteen-year-old summer camper in 1973, a
forester told him that there was nothing that could be done about the
slow death of trees in and around Los Angeles due to the toxic smog that
plagued the city. An idealist, Andy called on his fellow campers to dig up
an old parking lot and plant a meadow. He discovered that the California
Department of Forestry had surplus stock of eight thousand seedlings,
and he convinced them to turn them over to the teenager and his friends
for planting. Andy's project to "re-forest" Southern California began to
attract volunteers, funding, and press. He called his group TreePeople.

By 1977, TreePeople had recruited thousands of schoolchildren and
adult volunteers and had planted fifty thousand trees. When Los
Angeles was awarded the 1984 Summer Olympic Games, city officials

fretted that the infamous smog would hang over the event like a suffocating cloud. They proposed a twenty-year, $200 million project to plant one million trees. Andy told them that TreePeople could do the job in three years—at no cost to the city. Amazingly, four days before the lighting of the Olympic Flame, the one millionth tree—an apricot—was planted in a suburb of Los Angeles.

Today, TreePeople is recognized around the world for its educational programs, ecotours, and ongoing work to repair the environment. More than twenty thousand people support TreePeople and participate in an impressive array of campaigns and projects. Andy Lipkis, the young camper who refused to believe nothing could be done, has consulted with the White House; written a best-selling book, *The Simple Act of Planting a Tree*, with his wife, Kate; and visited China to share TreePeople's sustainability strategies.

Repairing the world—one tree at a time. See www.treepeople.org to learn more.

Going to the high school prom is a rite of passage for every teenager. For girls especially, it is a night to dress like Cinderella at the ball. But what if you cannot afford an expensive party dress, shoes, and accessories? In 2002, on both coasts of the United States, a group of women realized that there were hundreds of girls in this predicament. In Philadelphia, Joyce Jesko created a nonprofit organization called Fairy Godmothers (www.fairygodmothersinc.com) to collect gently used prom dresses from donors, which are then offered free to those who need them. In San Francisco, Laney Whitcanack and Kristi Smith Knutson sent an e-mail to friends looking for a prom dress for their teenage friend, Li Qiu. Eighty-five dresses were donated immediately, so Laney and Kristi established The Princess Project (www.princessproject.org) to provide prom dresses to teenagers in the Bay Area. In 2006, Marisa West, a seventeen-year-old teenager in Beltsville, Maryland, launched a project to collect prom dresses to send to the victims of Hurricane Katrina in Louisiana. All three projects collected more than a thousand prom dresses each!

One of the students who received a dress wrote this letter of thanks to Marisa:

Hi, I am a student at Cabrini high and in 11th grade. I lost everything in the storm; my home had 9 feet of water in it. I am soooo grateful that Miss West is doing this. All the students are so excited about the dresses and more than 100 are volunteering just to help. Some of the girls couldn't afford a dress, and many others were overstressed. This is really giving us a little sunshine in our lives after the storm. Thanks so much, Marisa West; words can't express how we feel. May God bless you and those who helped.

J. Dandridge, New Orleans

There are at least a dozen cities in America with volunteer groups working to ensure that every young woman can be properly dressed for her night at the ball.

Harold Schulweis is one of the great rabbis of his generation, a prophetic voice who has never sat silently in the face of injustice. In 2004, at the largest gathering of his congregation during the year, Rabbi Schulweis challenged his flock to do something about the growing genocide in Darfur. He recruited a dynamic lay leader, Janice Kamenir-Reznik, to head up the effort. They named the project Jewish World Watch. In short order, a variety of events were held to raise money to fund the creation of medical clinics and to dig water wells to aid the refugees fleeing the turmoil in Sudan. When they learned that women who ventured out of the camps to collect wood were being raped, Schulweis and Kamenir-Reznik bought hundreds of solar-heating stoves for cooking. Although the project emanated from one congregation—Valley Beth Shalom in Encino, California—forty local synagogues across Los Angeles established their own Jewish World Watch groups to raise funds and awareness. The result: thousands of people are being helped. See www.jewishworldwatch.org for more information.

Fixing the World, One Step at a Time

In his book *An Inconvenient Truth,* former vice president Al Gore warns that, far from repairing the world, we are actually destroying our planetary home. By ignoring the enormous increase in carbon dioxide emissions, we are heating up the globe at an alarming rate, causing havoc with the weather, melting the polar ice caps, and thereby threatening our very existence.

Be a repair person.

God forbid.

Mr. Gore is not the first to point out the importance of preserving God's gifts of nature. In a famous commentary on Ecclesiastes, we are warned:

> *God took the first human and, passing before all the trees of the Garden of Eden, said, "See My works, how fine and excellent they are! All that I created, I created for you. Consider that, and do not despoil or desolate My world; for if you destroy it, there will be no one to set it right after you."*
>
> KOHELET RABBAH 1, ON ECCLESIASTES 7:13

See God's works.

See the trees, the sky, the earth.

See human beings, made in the image of God.

Understand that you are one of the stewards of God's creation.

When you fix a small piece of the broken world, you are doing God's work.

God repairs.

Be a repair person.

God's To-Do List

 Repair

61. Be a giraffe—stick your neck out. Be a hero—find a new way to serve others in need.

62. Conserve water, plant trees and gardens, recycle, take care of the environment.

63. Turn off extra lights at home, use energy-conserving lightbulbs, and keep the thermostat at 68°F.

64. Reduce fuel consumption. Ride a bike. Walk. Use a more fuel-efficient vehicle.

65. Donate your wedding dress and prom dress to someone who can't afford one.

66. Be politically active—fight injustice wherever you see it.

67. Contribute time and money to social justice organizations.

68. Adopt a dog or cat from an animal shelter.

69. Build a lemonade stand, let your kids or kids in your community run it, and donate the money to a needy cause.

70. Travel to a country in need of volunteers and give of your spiritual gifts.

_____

_____

_____

_____

Wrestle 8

You can wrestle with God.

You can even argue with God.

In any serious relationship, there are times of struggle.

God doesn't mind a good fight.

Abraham is the first to argue with God.

The people of Sodom and Gomorrah, who failed to offer hospitality to Abraham's brother-in-law Lot when he pitched his tent near their cities, are called "very wicked sinners" (Gen. 13:13). Yet, when God tells Abraham of the decision to destroy Sodom, Abraham argues forcibly and eloquently with God:

> *Will You sweep away the innocent along with the guilty? What if there should be fifty innocent within the city; will You then wipe out the place and not forgive it for the sake of the innocent fifty who are in it? Far be it from You to do such a thing, to bring death upon the innocent as well as the guilty, so that innocent and guilty fare alike. Far be it from You! Shall not the Judge of all the earth deal justly?*
>
> GENESIS 18:23–25

You can wrestle with God.

This is breathtaking. The challenge is rooted in the audacious claim that even God is subject to the moral standards decreed for humans. One commentator suggests that this is not so much a question as a demand:

Do not exact strict justice upon these people! You, Lord, know how weak human nature is. You know how hard it is to be a good person in Sodom. Treat them more leniently than strict justice would require.

MESHEKH HOKHMAH

God responds by agreeing with Abraham: "If I find within the city of Sodom fifty innocent ones, I will forgive the whole place for their sake" (Gen. 18:26).

Abraham pushes the moral issue further: "Here I venture to speak to my Lord, I who am but dust and ashes: What if the fifty innocents should lack five? Will You destroy the whole city for want of the five?" (Gen. 18:27–28).

Once again, God agrees—no destruction if there are forty-five innocents in the city.

What if there are only forty? Abraham asks.

God agrees.

Thirty?

Yes.

Twenty?

Okay.

Abraham presses on: "Let not my Lord be angry if I speak but this last time: What if ten should be found there?" And God answers: "I will not destroy, for the sake of the ten" (Gen. 18:32).

In the end, there were not ten innocents in Sodom and Gommorah, and the cities were annihilated. But the spectacle of a man arguing so passionately with God became the theological basis for a commitment to social justice, and it set the model for a different kind of relationship between God and God's partners in the world.

Abraham argues; Jacob wrestles.

As a biblical hero, Jacob is a morally flawed man. With the encouragement of his mother, he cheats his older brother out of his birthright and tricks his father, Isaac, into giving his blessing to him instead of the intended recipient, Esau. Complicating matters, Esau is portrayed as a strong, fierce hunter guy, while Jacob is clearly a milquetoast momma's boy.

Imagine the scene, twenty years later, when Jacob prepares to encounter his brother. He is plenty nervous. He divides his camp in two, thinking one might survive the expected attack. He prays to God for deliverance. He sends presents ahead as a peace offering. On the night before the encounter, he sends his family across the Jabbok River, remaining alone, sleepless, restless, and worried. Suddenly, he is in a struggle:

> *And a man wrestled with him (Jacob) until the break of dawn. When he (the "man") saw that he had not prevailed against him, he wrenched Jacob's hip at its socket, so that the socket of his hip was strained as he wrestled with him.*
>
> GENESIS 32:25–26

Who was this mysterious being? A man? An angel? The spirit of Esau? Esau himself? An evil guardian of the river? God?

The answer may be in what happens next:

> *Then he (the "man") said: "Let me go, for dawn is breaking." But, he (Jacob) answered: "I will not let you go, unless you bless me." Said the other, "What is your name?" He replied: "Jacob." Said he: "Your name shall no longer be Jacob, but Yis-ra-El, for you have striven with beings divine and human, and have prevailed."*
>
> GENESIS 32:27–29

The changing of a name indicates a transformation in the character of Jacob, now Israel—the one who struggles with God. Whether the confrontation was with his demons, his conscience, or his God, Israel leaves the encounter forever changed. He is still concerned about his imminent meeting with his brother Esau, but there is a happy ending. According to the plain meaning of the text, "Esau ran to greet him, he embraced him and, falling on his neck, he kissed him; and they wept" (Gen. 33:4).

Godwrestling changes you forever.

The wrestling with God mirrors the rabbinic belief that every person constantly balances two opposing inclinations that shape behaviors and emotions: the *yetzer ha-ra*, the inclination to do evil, and the *yetzer ha-tov*, the inclination to do good. Jacob's wrestling match is about the struggle between his human tendency to run away from difficult situations and the spark of divinity within that would lead him to do the right thing. He crosses the river a transformed man, leaving his identity as Jacob—the cheater, liar, and trickster—and emerging as Israel, the one who faces up to God and people. There is a cost, of course, to the struggle; Israel is wounded, physically and emotionally, and he walks forward with a limp. Nevertheless, the Bible later describes him, arriving at the city of Shechem, as *shalem*—whole (a variant of the word *shalom*).

There are times in life when you wrestle with God.

Godwrestling

I have been bereaved, but I have not yet been a mourner. As contradictory as that sounds, it is true. I have lost a child, but I have not mourned her.

Susie and I were married for three years before we got pregnant. I say "we" because throughout the uneventful pregnancy, I felt as close to the baby-to-be as a father could. I marveled at every stage of development during the nine months, especially when the baby moved. What an amazing feeling it is to touch a human being *in potentia* within the womb! A leg or an arm would push out from Susie's belly, seemingly anxious to come out and play. Pregnancy is a time of great excitement and wonderful dreams about what will be. Will it be a girl or boy? Will she or he look like Susie or me? What will we name the child? How will having a child change our lives? We had taken Lamaze childbirth classes and awaited the due date. The superstitions about setting up a nursery notwithstanding, we had ordered the basic furniture and bought a few toys. We hadn't thought for even an instant about the possibility that something could go wrong, terribly wrong.

Our first child was born full term on the afternoon of May 6, 1974, and died thirteen hours later. The baby had become stressed during a prolonged labor, and Susie was rushed into an emergency cesarean section. Due to the stress, the baby had ingested contaminated embryonic fluid, a medical condition known as meconium aspiration. Despite the valiant efforts of a team of neonatal specialists throughout the night, there was no way to save her.

The baby had been rushed from the delivery room to the neonatal intensive care unit of Children's Hospital, across the street from Barnes

Hospital where Susie remained. Susie's parents stayed with her, and I waited through the night at Children's with my parents. The doctors and nurses were superb, bringing us updates on the baby's condition, but holding out little hope. At one point, a social worker suggested I see the baby. It was a heart-wrenching moment. I spent most of the night crying, thinking about Susie and how devastating this loss would be for her. Susie had spent the night recovering from the operation in the last room at the end of the hall on the maternity floor. The first inkling she had that something was wrong came when a nurse walked into the room and took down several decorative pictures of smiling mothers holding their newborns. I talked to her by phone, admitting that there was a problem, suggesting that she try to rest from the ordeal of the labor and operation.

Early in the morning, a terrific young intern who had worked all night on the case came into the waiting room to give me the news, but his crying eliminated the need for words. The shock overwhelmed me, even though I knew it was coming. I literally ran across the street to the hospital wing where Susie had been taken. "She died" were the only words I could get out before collapsing into her arms. We cried together for a long time at this most unhappy ending. Little did I know that the ordeal had just begun.

No one knew how to handle this tragedy—no one. The nurses moved Susie from the maternity floor to the urology ward to save her the pain of hearing the sounds of babies. The obstetrician came to say he was sorry and then warned us that, because he had had to do a C-section, he would have to add $350 to his fee. Our parents, expecting their first grandchild, were devastated. Our friends rushed to the hospital to offer comfort, but most only exacerbated the hurt with comments like: "You're young. You'll have other children." "It'll be okay." Well, it was definitely not okay. What should have been a moment of supreme joy had become the ultimate nightmare. Instead of rejoicing as new parents, we were plunged into intense grief.

For Susie, the loss was overwhelming. She was feeling enormous sadness, anger, and pain. Despite the assurances of doctors, social workers, and me that we would recover, Susie felt unheard and abandoned. I refused to mourn, a terrible mistake. Instead, I spent sleepless nights worrying about Susie and dealing with questions of faith. Why did this happen? How could God let this innocent baby die? As much as our family and community rallied to support us, in the depths of the night, we wrestled with God, emerging from the experience wounded but hopeful.

We moved to Los Angeles and came under the care of a wonderful doctor specializing in high-risk pregnancies. It took two years for us to get pregnant again—two years of unresolved mourning for Susie and two years of denial for me. After a very carefully monitored pregnancy, we celebrated the birth of our daughter Havi Michele. Two years later, Michael Louis was born.

Seven years after the death of our first baby, Susie joined MEND (Mothers Experiencing Neonatal Death), a support group for mothers dealing with this tragedy, and finally began to resolve her grief. She began to counsel other grieving parents, something she is called on to do all too often. To this day, I feel I have never truly mourned the loss of our first baby. To this day, we struggle to understand why this happened to us.

The biblical stories teach that God does not shut down protest, disagreement, or argument. God created a world in which humans have free will, a world that is not at all perfect, a world where bad things do happen to good people and natural disasters occur with unfortunate frequency. Do not fear asking questions and confronting God with the injustices you find. Don't worry; God can handle it.

Godwrestling changes you forever.

Kathy and Dennis Gura have wrestled with God.

Their daughter Rebecca was seventeen months old when she was diagnosed with leukemia. She was six years old when she died. According to Kathy and Dennis, Rebecca wanted to make it to her sixth birthday.

The first thing out of the mouth of the social worker when the parents learned their daughter had cancer was, "You know, 80 percent of the parents who go through this end up divorced." Kathy and Dennis were determined that wouldn't happen, for Rebecca's sake at least.

Dennis reflects on the experience: "Oh, we had our fights. You can't imagine how intense it is to fight cancer for four years. Counseling helped. But, really, our commitment to Rebecca, to each other, and to keeping our family together was most important. Lots of friends who had kids the same age dropped out of our lives when they learned that Rebecca had cancer. I guess it was just too scary for them. And I'm sure our anger drove away others. Those friends who stayed close to us tended to be those with a religious commitment. Of course, our synagogue community was fantastic. People would offer to do things for us, little things, but they meant a lot. The first Shabbat we were in the hospital friends brought us candles and wine, so we could make Shabbat there, in the protective isolation unit."

Dennis and Kathy asked the inevitable question: "Why is this happening to us?" "Has God abandoned us?" "How can God allow a child, an innocent child, to die such a horrible death?"

Somehow, even through the struggle, they held on to their belief in God. It helped to know that they were not alone. The world is full of Godwrestlers.

"Sometimes Kathy and I feel like we haven't grown one day older since the day Rebecca died. Somehow, a part of us died that day, too. On the other hand, I'm reminded of the Hasidic story of the woman whose child died; she is in incredible grief. She goes to the rebbe and asks him what to do. He says: 'Bake a cake.' 'What?' she asks. 'Bake a cake, but use only flour you borrow from those whose pain is less than yours. Bring it to me next *Shabbos.*' Shabbat comes and the lady returns to the rebbe empty-handed. 'Where is the cake?' he asks. She says: 'I couldn't get the flour, for there was no one with less pain in their lives than me.'"

In the book *A Time to Mourn, a Time to Comfort: A Guide to Jewish Bereavement and Comfort* (Jewish Lights), Rabbi Jack Reimer observes the resilience of human beings who have wrestled with God:

> The real wonder of Adam and Eve is that they lost two children—Cain and Abel—in one fell swoop, and then the Bible says, "And Adam made love to his wife again." It teaches us that when you sustain a loss, you get up off your knees and start all over again. Otherwise, we'd all be descended from a murderer or from a victim. Adam and Eve taught us how to love, and lose, and love again.
>
> Noah gets off the ark and gets drunk. I never understood why he did that until I talked with a Holocaust survivor. He said, "I understand Noah.

I did the same thing. I came home and everything was swept away. Every house, every friend, every relative. I got into a drunken stupor too, because I didn't want to live. Eventually, I woke up again, but I understood what Noah did."

Aaron loses two children on the day of his investiture. Moses tries to give him some religious cliché for comfort, and Aaron just looks at him. And the Bible—which doesn't waste words—indicates that Aaron was silent. He could have blasphemed, but he didn't. He could have gone on as if nothing had happened, but God is not so hard up that God needs praise from people who don't mean it. What Aaron did instead was to withdraw, to nurse his wounds, and when he was ready and able to come back, he did.

At the end of the Book of Job, after Job has lost everything, it says that he had seven more children. I once heard Archibald MacLeish say that this is the whole point of the book. Having lost seven children, God planted in Job the courage, the resilience to be willing to risk again and have more children.

The most recent example of this ability to recover from loss is a passage from modern Jewish history. From 1945 to 1948, Jews who survived World War II lived in what is correctly called a "Displaced Persons" camp. They couldn't go back to Poland—it was contaminated. They couldn't go to Palestine—the doors were locked. They couldn't get to America. So they were cooped up for three years in Displaced Persons camps. During those three years, these broken people—shards of people, widows, widowers, mourners—found each other, married, and brought children into the world. There were more children born in those three years than in any other period for which we have Jewish demographic records. You hear a lot of talk from people who aren't sure whether they want to bring children into this world. If our parents had waited until it was a good time to bring children into the world, we'd have a much smaller Jewish community today. They loved, and lost, and risked again—just as Job did. There is no theological justification for evil or suffering—just a response. And the response we learn from Adam, Aaron, Job, and the Holocaust survivors is: Try again.

Facing the Challenge

You may be wrestling with the inevitable challenges in your life. You may have been in an abusive relationship and wrestling with that. You may be in a financial reversal and wrestling with that. You or someone you love may be ill and wrestling with that. You may be struggling with an addiction and wrestling with that. You may be in trouble with your marriage and wrestling with that. You may be worrying about your kids and wrestling with that. You may be wondering how to care for your elderly parents and wrestling with that.

There is no doubt that there are many moments of wrestling in life. The question is: will you trust that God will be there with you through the struggle and lead you to a life of blessing?

Will you trust that God will be there with you through the struggle and lead you to a life of blessing?

God could easily pin you in a wrestling match. But that's not the way God works. God welcomes your struggle and will stand with you, hand in hand. The question remains: can you come out of the struggle like Jacob/Israel, transformed for the better, even if you limp?

God's To-Do List

 Wrestle

71. Praise God, but don't be afraid to question, too.

72. Recognize that the struggle between your inclination to do bad and your inclination to do good is natural. Everyone has bad thoughts; good people don't act on them.

73. Find a cause where people are wrestling and work for it.

74. Don't get crazy if someone says, "I don't believe in God." He or she is Godwrestling.

75. If people "damn" God, be sympathetic to their struggle. They are Godwrestling.

76. Fight for the underdog.

77. Practice the art of compromise.

78. When you wrestle with problems in the middle of the night, remember that God will be there with you.

79. Learn how to argue with your loved ones, lovingly. Listen!

80. Ask someone from your spiritual community to be an angel and help you struggle through an especially tough wrestling match.

_____

_____

_____

_____

Give

God gives. And God teaches how to give.

The people of the Bible believed this. Consider the story of the Israelite slaves, liberated from Egypt, wandering in the desert for forty years. The food they brought from Egypt had run out. What would they eat?

> *The Lord spoke to Moses: "I have heard the grumbling of the Israelites. Speak to them and say: 'By evening you shall eat flesh, and in the morning you shall have your fill of bread; and you shall know that I the Lord am your God.'" In the evening quail appeared and covered the camp. When the fall of dew lifted, there, over the surface of the wilderness, lay a fine and flaky substance, as fine as frost on the ground. When the Israelites saw it, they said to one another, "What is it?"—for they did not know what it was. And Moses said to them: "That is the bread which the Lord has given you to eat.... The house of Israel named it manna.*
>
> EXODUS 16:11–15, 31

The memory of this act of giving reverberates throughout the Bible. In a remarkable instruction received in God's Word at Sinai, the people are told always to leave a corner of the field, filled with produce, for the poor of the community.

> *"Just as God provided you manna in the desert, you shall provide food for the needy...."*
>
> LEVITICUS 19:9–10

It is a broken world when children go to bed hungry, when the homeless stand on street corners and beg for food, when millions in Third World countries die of malnutrition and starvation.

God entrusted humankind with a world of boundless bounty. The United States alone produces enough food to feed the world. Why, then, is there still a plague of hunger?

There is no reason that anyone in the world should go hungry. Yet, millions of children and adults go to bed every night with empty stomachs.

This cannot be. You must be God's agent on earth and ensure that no one suffers from hunger.

God's Hands

Judy and Beryl went out to dinner at The Cheesecake Factory, a restaurant known for serving large portions of food. At the end of the meal, Judy suddenly ordered another entrée. Beryl thought she was taking it home to someone. In a way, she was. Just outside the front door of the place, a homeless man sat asking for help. Judy handed him the bag of food. She had noticed him when she arrived at the restaurant. The man smiled, looked up at her, and said: "God bless you."

Don Greenberg gives peaches to his friends and family. Every summer since he retired from his wholesale produce business eighteen years ago, Don contacts a carefully selected peach supplier who grows a rare variety of O'Henry peaches the size of softballs. When ripened, the enormous peach oozes sweet juice with extraordinary flavor. In his hometown, you are considered fortunate indeed to be on Don's list of nearly two hundred people who get a half-case or more of the delicacy.

Usually, Don delivers the peaches to his list, loading eighty-eight cases into his car. Last summer, Don had major surgery and was physically restricted. So, he sent an e-mail to his list, announcing the arrival of the peaches and when they could be picked up from his home. The scene is like some sort of adult Halloween, car after car of friends coming by to get "Papa Don's Peaches." They are thrilled to receive the gift, a moment eagerly anticipated all year long. Why does he do it? Don says: "You can't find these peaches anywhere else in the world. I want people to experience something unusual And, it's fun to give them away to my list, plus I know that they will, in turn, give some of the peaches to their family and friends." So, the giving grows.

This is one of my favorite stories, based on a classic Jewish folktale, retold beautifully by Rabbi Ed Feinstein:

Once, many years ago, in a small village, there lived two Jews. Reb Chaim was the richest man in the town, and Reb Yankel the poorest.

Every Friday evening, Reb Chaim would come to the synagogue in his fine Shabbat coat and his exquisite fur hat. As the service ended, he strode up the hill to his magnificent mansion. His butler met him at the door and showed him into the regal dining room where a table fit for a king awaited him. He was served the most remarkable Shabbat meal accompanied by the sweetest, most heavenly challah (special egg bread). But none of it brought Reb Chaim joy. For he was alone. Reb Chaim had no family.

Reb Chaim suddenly realized what he needed—he needed to share his Shabbat feast with someone. But with whom? "Who is worthy of sharing my Shabbat feast?" he wondered. "Only God!" he decided. "Let God share my wonderful Shabbat feast." He told his baker: "Next week, I would like you to make me two extra challahs."

The next Shabbat, Reb Chaim entered the synagogue before anyone and walked to the Holy Ark. He stood for a moment in prayer. "Master of the Universe, each week I enjoy a magnificent Shabbat feast. This week, I want You, God, to share my feast. So I have brought you challahs. Even You God have never tasted challah so good!" With that, Reb Chaim opened the Ark and tucked the challahs behind the Torah scrolls.

Reb Yankel also went to the synagogue on Friday night, but he always arrived late and always sat in the very back. It had been a bad week, a bad month, a bad season. Each week Yankel's family had less and less to eat. And tonight, he couldn't bring himself to face his children over an empty

Shabbat table. So he sat in the synagogue as everyone left. When he was alone, he walked to the Holy Ark, stood a few minutes, and offered his prayer: "Master of the World, how can You make me go home to see my children hungry? Without Your help, God, I refuse to leave the synagogue!" With that, he slammed his hands on the doors of the Holy Ark. The Ark opened up, and out rolled two beautiful, golden, warm challahs.

"It's a miracle!" screamed Reb Yankel, "Thank You, dear God, thank You!"

He ran home and placed the challahs on the family table.

"Where did you get such rich challah?" asked his wife.

"It was a gift, a miracle of God, an answer to my prayers. Now let us eat and celebrate!"

It would be difficult to measure where there was greater joy that Friday night—in the tiny, poor home of Reb Yankel, whose children had never eaten challah so sweet, or in the mansion of Reb Chaim, who ate and drank and sang his prayers with a new spirit.

So the following week, Reb Chaim again ordered his baker to make two challahs, and again he placed them in the Holy Ark, saying, "Dear God, thank You for accepting my gifts." At the end of the service, when the synagogue was empty, Reb Yankel again humbly approached the Holy Ark. "Master of the World, I have come to give thanks for the joy You brought my family last week. Is it possible I could ask for another miracle?" And with that, he timidly opened the Ark, and out rolled two more golden challahs!

This went on for a full month. And another. And another. Until a whole year of challahs had gone by. Each week, Reb Chaim filled the Ark with his gifts for God. And each week, Reb Yankel accepted God's miracles. It was the greatest year in each man's life.

As the year came to an end, a terrible thing happened. The caretaker who cleaned the synagogue saw Reb Chaim, the richest man in the town, approach the Holy Ark carrying two challahs and put them in the Ark before the service. And he saw Reb Yankel, the poorest man in town, take the challahs from the Ark after the service. He rushed after both men and brought them back to the synagogue.

"Fools," the caretaker ridiculed them. "You, Reb Chaim, do you really think that God eats your challah each week? It is this beggar who takes from you! And you, Reb Yankel, do you really believe that God hears your prayers and miraculously feeds your family?! It is this miser!" The spirits of both Reb Chaim and Reb Yankel shriveled within them as they realized there was no miracle.

Now the rabbi heard what had happened and summoned all three men to his study. The rabbi sat at his desk, staring into a holy book, shaking his head, and groaning in sadness. "Do you know that this miracle was foreseen since the creation of the world? It was God's special joy to see it renewed each week. Your hands were God's hands. How will the miracle be repaired?"

Looking at one another for the first time, Reb Chaim and Reb Yankel knew what the rabbi meant. The following Friday night, instead of opening the doors of the Ark to place his challahs, Reb Chaim opened his doors to the family of Reb Yankel, and they, in turn, filled his home with song and spirit.

Then the rabbi turned his powerful gaze to the caretaker. "You are a cruel and evil man. Now hear your punishment: You will leave this town tonight, and you will wander the world. And you will tell everyone you meet the story of the miracle of Reb Chaim and Reb Yankel. And when you die, your children will tell the story. And when they die, their children will tell the story. Until everyone in every corner of the world has heard the story. In that way, you, too, will repair the miracle."

And now, dear reader, you, too, have heard the story.

Giving from the Heart

There is giving … and then there is giving from the heart.

The Bible makes it clear that human beings can be reluctant to give. In fact, when it came time to take a census of the people, God tells Moses to require that every person over the age of twenty give a half-shekel to be used ultimately in the building of the portable Tabernacle in the desert.

This is what everyone who is entered in the records shall pay: a half-shekel.... the rich shall not pay more and the poor shall not pay less....

EXODUS 30:13, 15

Yet, God also tells Moses to accept gifts "from every person whose heart so moves him *(yidvenu libo)*" (Exod. 25:2). In another instance, the call is to give "gifts to the Lord—everyone whose heart so moves him *(kol n'div libo)*" (Exod. 35:5).

How do you give from the heart?

You give willingly. You give not only material gifts, but also the gift of a willing heart.

The Bible weighs in on this explicitly:

If there is a needy person among you, one of your kinsmen in any of your settlements in the land that the Lord your God is giving you, do not harden your heart and shut your hand against your needy kinsman. Rather, you must open your hand and lend him sufficient for whatever he needs.

DEUTERONOMY 15:7–8

God knows that when the heart is hardened, the hand is closed. When the heart is hard, you become indifferent to the needs of others. When the heart is open, you see the other person differently. You don't see the homeless person on the street as a lazy vagabond. You see a human being, made in the image of God.

When you open your heart and let the love come out, you open your hand.

> **When you open your heart and let the love come out, you open your hand.**

When you give, you take.

You take in the knowledge that your loving gift will make something good happen.

You take into your heart a sense of generosity of spirit.

When you give, you are not diminished. Quite the contrary. Your heart is filled with gratitude that your contribution has made a difference.

Giving from the heart means giving with love.

Our children learned a song in kindergarten, a version of "Magic Penny" by Malvina Reynolds, that I have always thought so profound in its simplicity:

> *Love is something if you give it away, give it away, give it away.*
> *Love is something if you give it away—it comes right back to you.*
> *It's just like a magic penny,*
> *Hold it tight and you won't have any.*
> *Lend it, spend it, give it away—*
> *It comes right back to you.*
> *Love is something if you give it away, give it away, give it away.*
> *Love is something if you give it away—it comes right back to you.*

When our daughter Havi turned thirty years old, we celebrated with a small dinner party at home. The big day happened to fall on a Friday, so we invited family and several of Havi's friends to join us in our home for our usual Shabbat meal, with the twist of birthday cake for dessert. Havi's ninety-five-year-old grandfather, Zadie K., made the trip from Omaha to California; he has never missed one of Havi's thirty birthdays.

Earlier, I had called Havi's brother Michael in New York and offered to send him a ticket to join the celebration in Los Angeles. "Oh, Dad," he said with a sadness in his voice, "I'm just so busy at work. I couldn't possibly get away."

The evening was glorious. As Havi sliced into the birthday cake, there was a knock on the door. Standing there was Lucy, one of Michael's friends from high school. And, right behind Lucy, was Michael! He had arranged to come as a surprise—not only for Havi, but also for Zadie K., Susie, and me. All manner of screaming ensued while brother embraced sister and wished her a happy birthday with one of the best gifts ever—his presence.

Giving your self can be the greatest gift of all.

Be a Messenger

Before our first trip to Israel, the most amazing thing happened.

I was telling a friend that Susie and I were leaving in a week, and suddenly, he pulled out his wallet, took out a $1 bill, and handed it to me.

"This is for *tzedakah* (charity)," he said. "Find someone who needs it. Now, you are a *shaliach mitzvah*—a mitzvah messenger. God will protect you."

I understood immediately. My trip now had an extra-special goal, a task that elevated the experience from a vacation to a journey with a sacred purpose.

I folded the dollar bill carefully and stuck it in a corner of my wallet—and in a corner of my heart. I thought about it constantly—who would I find that needed the dollar? How would it feel when I finally gave it?

On a street in Jerusalem, I saw her. She was an old woman, dressed in tattered clothes, sitting on the stone pavement in the corner of an alleyway. Her teeth had rotted away, and her hair was tangled under a worn scarf. She mumbled something in Hebrew as I approached, palm extended, an anxious look in her eyes. I took out my wallet and retrieved the dollar bill that my friend had charged me to deliver to someone in need. I handed her the dollar and her eyes brightened. She took it quickly and squirreled it away in her clothing. She said nothing, but I did: "*Todah,*" I whispered. "Thank you." I walked away on a cloud, grateful that my mission had been accomplished, privileged that God had watched over me and blessed me to do this good deed, this small act of kindness.

Everyone involved in that moment was doing God's work. I fulfilled the obligation to complete the task I was given. My friend, the donor of the dollar, not only performed the mitzvah of giving, but he also did the mitzvah of making my journey meaningful. And, although she didn't realize it, the poor woman had received a gift from an anonymous donor; I was only the *shaliach* (messenger). Of all the donations I have made in my life, giving that dollar bill was the most meaningful one of all.

Be an angel-messenger. Take a dollar bill out of your purse or wallet. Right now—don't wait. Put it into an envelope. Write the words "God Bless You" on the envelope. Give the envelope to a family member or a friend. Ask her or him to be your angel-messenger and find someone or some cause to give it to. Pay it forward. And when you see a needy person, or you learn about a worthy cause, give. It will do good, and it will feel good. Make the act of giving a regular way that you do God's work.

Giving Is Life

In the Land of Israel, there are two large bodies of water. In the north, there is a large lake called the Sea of Galilee. It is teeming with fish, and people enjoy its breezes. The Jordan River feeds it in the northern end and then continues its journey to the south. There is another body of water in the southern desert. It has no life in it, it smells like sulfur, and no one lives around it. The Jordan River flows into it, but does not flow out.

Giving your self can be the greatest gift of all.

What is the difference between these two bodies of water?

The Sea of Galilee gives and lives.

This other sea gives nothing. It is named the Dead Sea.

Just as there are two seas in Israel, so there are two kinds of people in the world.

Sir Winston Churchill said: "We make a living by what we get, we make a life by what we give."

Give of your God-given gifts as you do God's To-Do List.

God's To-Do List

 Give

81. What is your passion? What are you good at? Use your talents to serve others.

82. Give anonymously. Have flowers delivered to your local senior centers.

83. Give someone the gift of learning: tutor a child in your neighborhood, or lend someone a book you love.

84. Give of your time—it is your most precious commodity. Volunteer. Check out www.usafreedomcorps.gov (United States government volunteer opportunities), www.pointsoflight.org, or your local congregation for ideas on how to get involved in a good cause.

85. Enjoy the gift of giving. Give generously of your resources with a full heart.

86. Create a shelf in your pantry to store cans designated for the local food bank or a food drive.

87. Put an alms box or container next to your bed. Empty your pockets of change every night. Contribute the money to a worthy cause.

88. Give away to the needy the things you would sell on eBay; donate old clothes to a homeless shelter.

89. Surprise someone with your presence.

90. Give blood.

_____

_____

_____

10
Forgive

It may be the most difficult thing a human being is asked to do: forgive someone for doing something wrong.

God forgives.

In the Bible, the most dramatic example of God's forgiveness is the experience at Mount Sinai. Moses has led the People Israel out of Egypt and into the desert. When they reach the foot of the mountain, Moses climbs it to have the ultimate encounter with God. There, on the mountaintop, Moses receives the Ten Commandments directly from God. They are inscribed on two tablets of stone, written by "the finger of God."

Moses spends forty days and forty nights on the mountain. Meanwhile, the people are restless and fear that their leader has disappeared. They create an idol, a Golden Calf, to which they sacrifice and pray. God tells Moses what has happened and threatens to destroy the people.

> The Lord ... said to Moses: "I see that this is a stiff-necked people. Now,
> let Me be, that My anger may blaze forth against them and that I may
> destroy them, and make of you a great nation."
>
> EXODUS 32:9

In other words, God intends to wipe out the Israelites and start anew with the descendants of Moses. But Moses will have none of it. He implores God:

> Let not Your anger, O Lord, blaze forth against Your people, whom you
> delivered from the land of Egypt with great power and a mighty hand. Let
> not the Egyptians say, "It was with evil intent that He delivered them,
> only to kill them off in the mountains and annihilate them from the face

of the earth." Turn from Your blazing anger, and renounce the plan to punish Your people. Remember Your servants, Abraham, Isaac, and Jacob, how You swore to them by Your Self and said to them "I will make your offspring as numerous as the stars of heaven, and I will give to your offspring this whole land of which I spoke, to possess forever."

EXODUS 32:11–13

And so God forgives.

And the Lord renounced the punishment He planned to bring upon His people.

EXODUS 32:14

Yet, when Moses actually sees the people idolizing the Golden Calf, he throws the tablets to the ground, shattering them into pieces. Moses is angry, but he realizes that he must intercede with God to reestablish the covenant:

You have been guilty of a great sin. Yet, I will now go up to the Lord, perhaps I may win forgiveness for your sin. Moses went back to the Lord and said, "Alas, this people is guilty of a great sin in making for themselves a god of gold. Now, if You will forgive their sin (well and good); but, if not, erase me from the record which You have written!"

EXODUS 32:30–32

God tells Moses that the people who sinned will be punished, but God instructs Moses to lead the people to the Promised Land. Moreover, God tells Moses to carve two new tablets and prepare for a second giving of the Ten Commandments. In one of the most beautiful of biblical passages, God proclaims the characteristics of forgiveness:

If God is capable of forgiving, so are you.

The Lord! The Lord! a God compassionate and gracious, slow to anger, abounding in kindness and faithfulness, extending kindness to the thousandth generation, forgiving iniquity, transgression, and sin ...

EXODUS 34:6–7

If God is capable of forgiving, so are you.

It's not easy to forgive a wrong.

In Jewish tradition, a wrong is reflected in the Hebrew term *chet,* often translated as "sin," but it really means "missing the mark."

You aim to be good. Your intentions are good. And yet, the effort gets sidetracked, off-line, twisted. People are hurt; sometimes, the people closest to you. You always hurt the ones you love.

The act of *teshuvah*—often translated as "repentance," but it really means "return"—is an ultimate value in Judaism. An entire High Holy Day season is devoted to it, beginning with the *selichot,* prayers that ask for forgiveness, pledge a return to good works, and remind us that human beings are capable of godliness.

> You must ask the one whom you've wronged for forgiveness.
>
> And the one who is wronged must offer it.

Yet, all the confessional pleas in the world to God cannot replace the one act of courage without which there is no true repentance, no real re-turning.

You must ask the one whom you've wronged for forgiveness.

And the one who is wronged must offer it.

This process of human reconciliation is one of the most difficult things to do on God's To-Do List. Yet, by tapping the reservoir of divinity within, you can do it. You can ask for forgiveness. And you can forgive.

Asking for Forgiveness

In the Jewish tradition, words alone cannot right a wrong. There are six steps to seeking forgiveness:

1. Stop doing it. Whatever it is that you are doing or have done that has caused harm, you've got to stop it. Asking for forgiveness begins with actions, not words.
2. Recognize that what you've done is wrong. This requires self-reflection and understanding of your motives and actions. It's one thing for someone

to tell you that what you've done is wrong; it's quite another to realize it yourself.

3. Feel remorse for your actions. This is what infuriates wronged people at trials—the perpetrator offers no feelings of regret, failure, despair, or sadness. If you truly seek forgiveness, say you're sorry.

4. Make good. If you have harmed another by stealing money, pay it back. If you have damaged someone's reputation unfairly, do everything you can to repair it.

5. Confess. There is public confession during prayer, particularly during the holiday of Yom Kippur, the Day of Atonement. Personal confession, expressed in the prayers of *Al Chet,* can be offered before God and during private prayer.

6. Ask for forgiveness. Approach the wronged person and ask for forgiveness. Several times, if necessary. It will likely be necessary.

This process is not easy. Yet, if you truly want to ask for forgiveness from someone, doing these six steps of *teshuvah* with a sincere heart will prepare the way.

Forgiving

As challenging as it is to ask for forgiveness, it is just as difficult, perhaps more difficult, to forgive.

There is no "easy" forgiveness in Judaism. Only if the person seeking forgiveness is serious—and does the six steps of *teshuvah* to demonstrate that seriousness—is the person deemed *deserving* of forgiveness.

Even then, the tradition understands that there are different levels of forgiveness.

The first, *mechila,* relieves the offender of his or her debt. It is like a pardon granted to a felon who has served time and offered restitution—"you've paid your debt to me and society, but the crime remains."

The second, *selicha,* is forgiveness from the heart. It comes from a deep understanding of human frailty and a willingness to offer sympathy.

The third, *kappara,* is atonement—ultimate forgiveness—granted only by God.

Rabbi Harold Schulweis sees families whose members do not speak to each other: parents who do not speak to their children, children who do not speak to their parents, and siblings who do not speak to each other. In a sermon entitled "Forgiveness and Reconciliation" delivered on Rosh Hashanah in 2000, he offered these words of wisdom about forgiveness:

The telephone rings in my study. Papa has died. Arrangements for the funeral must be made.

"I would like to meet with the entire family," I say. The voice on the other end is silent.

"That's not going to be easy, Rabbi," she says.

"Why? Are they not in town?"

"They are in town, all right. But the boys haven't spoken to each other for over ten years. And that goes for their children. They won't sit in the same room together."

"But, it's their father," I reply.

The other voice says, "I know."

I meet with the boys, their wives and their children—separately. Not together. At the funeral, the brothers and their respective families sit separately, not together, not in the family room, but on separate benches in separate rows. Why? How did it start? When did it start? When I ask the origin of the anger, I discover that no one in the family remembers what caused the impasse. No one knows its genesis, but the deadlock continues without end....

Our tradition knows that I am not perfect. I am not unblemished, flawless. I have sins to confess and for which I seek forgiveness.

And you, whom do you forgive? Do you think that forgiveness is only God's affair? Do you think prayer runs only vertically—up to down?

The Talmud won't allow that: "Those transgressions between God and the individual, the Day of Atonement atones for; but those transgressions between the individual and her/his fellow human being, the Day of Atonement does not forgive, unless one personally appeases the other and seeks forgiveness."

But, in Judaism, the purpose of prayer is not the adulation of God, but the imitation of God. Not the admiration of God, but the emulation of God's ways. God is the ideal, the model to be emulated by me in my life horizontally—between me and you, and my family and friends—brother, sister, son, daughter. The Rabbis spelled out the moral correlation: "As God is merciful, be thou merciful. As God is compassionate, be thou compassionate. As God forgives, you forgive."

I know what you're thinking. "Poor innocent, naïve rabbi. Do you know what he did to me? What she said? How they plotted? How can I forgive? How can I forget what he-she-they did?"

Hold on, dear friend. Did anyone ever ask you to *forget*? What has forgiveness got to do with forgetting? Where is it written that when God forgives your sin, God thereby forgets your sin? Judaism is a reality-based faith. To forgive is not to forget; to forgive is to be liberated from inner anger, from the quest for vengeance that consumes your life and embitters the life of your family. To forgive is not to forget. No one expects you to forget. No one believes that forgiveness eliminates the memory of the pain and anguish of the injury....

You cannot turn back the clock. Forgiveness does not reverse the past, but it promises a new and different outcome. When you forgive, when you seek reconciliation, things may never be as they were before the injury. But, you can establish a new relationship, a speaking, civil relationship....

Seize the moment. Break the impasse. Break down the anger. Break through the stubbornness. Overcome the ugliness of past history. Open your heart, open your mouth. Initiate the first call. Initiate the first piercing of the wall of silence. Reconcile. Bend.

Reconciliation is hard. It requires a measure of heroism and sacrifice. Sacrifice is always associated with atonement. In ancient times, and in modern times, there is always sacrifice. Love costs. Forgiveness costs. Reconciliation costs. Peace costs. Family costs. Swallow your pride. Bury your stubbornness. Sacrifice.

Reconciliation carries risk. What if the person you seek to appease doesn't answer, remains obdurate? The sage Maimonides in the Mishnah

Torah urges us to seek appeasement again, again, and again. And if the other remains stubborn after three attempts, only then may you leave him or her alone. The one who refuses to reconcile is now the sinner. He or she is considered cruel.

This takes personal courage. Our sages asked: "Who is a hero?" The answer: "He who makes an enemy into a friend, an adversary into an ally." You can find a hundred reasons for not reaching out. But, reaching out begins now. Look into the eyes of the other—papa, mama, son, daughter, brother, sister, friend. Did we not hear the same song today— the words of the prophet Jeremiah?

> *Is not Ephraim my beloved son, my beloved child?*
> *Even when I speak against him, I remember him with affection.*
> *Therefore, my heart yearns for him.*
> *I will surely have compassion.*
>
> JEREMIAH 31:20

Extend your hand. Embrace the other. Heal the pain.
God forgives. God seeks reconciliation.
Dare we not?

Carol has a sister, Diane, who did a terrible wrong to her many, many years ago. They have been estranged ever since. Last year, Diane lay dying in a hospital room in Chicago. She called Carol in New York to let her know the situation. "I am deeply sorry for what I did, and I want to see you before I die." Carol put down the phone and began to sob. Could she forgive Diane? She took the next plane to Chicago and rushed to Diane's bedside. The two sisters embraced for the first time in forty years. Diane whispered: "Please forgive me. I was wrong." Carol wiped her tears away and said: "I forgive you. I am sorry it has taken us so long to reach this moment. I've missed you in my life."

"I've missed you, too," Diane sobbed. "And now, we have so little time."

In the two weeks that followed, the two sisters spent hour upon hour telling each other about their life's journeys, reminiscing about the good times before their conflict, noticing their similarities—they were sisters, after all. When the time came, Carol closed Diane's eyes and kissed her one final good-bye. After the funeral, she said that she was sure that Diane had held on to life in order to have this time of forgiveness with her and that she felt like a huge boulder had been removed from her heart.

Forgiving Yourself

Asking for forgiveness and forgiving require one crucial prerequisite: *Forgiving yourself.*

You are not perfect. You weren't created to be perfect.

King Solomon said:

> *There is no righteous person on earth who does only good and does not sin.*
> ECCLESIASTES 7:20

It's not easy.

So, you goofed up. And you've asked for forgiveness from the one you have wronged. And he or she forgave you.

But now, you can't forgive yourself. You feel guilty. You are emotionally paralyzed. You play it over and over again in your head. It weighs upon your heart. You cannot face yourself in the mirror.

Give yourself a break. God knows, you must forgive yourself to move on.

The Night of Forgiveness, the Day of Atonement

When I was a child, the High Holy Day of Yom Kippur was a time of mystery, honesty, and spirituality. In the synagogue of my youth, I would enter through the back vestibule, which was lined with memorial plaques with the names of dearly departed. Next to each name was a small light-bulb, which was usually turned on only on the anniversary of the person's death. But on *Kol Nidrei* (the Yom Kippur evening prayer) night, every single lightbulb was illuminated, creating an eerie glow that filled the sanctuary with the memory of souls we loved.

To this day, I love Yom Kippur. It is my favorite holiday. There is something absolutely transformative about the day. It is the culmination of the Ten Days of Renewal, ten days of reflecting on my life and my purpose.

On Yom Kippur, I am just a little lower than the angels. In fact, all of the spiritual practices of the day are designed to help me focus on my soul, not my body—to elevate me from my animal existence to something higher. On Yom Kippur, I spend almost the entire day in the synagogue immersed in prayer, study, and reflection. I don't eat or drink. I don't wear leather, a sign of luxury, and I don't wear a watch.

A neighbor of mine goes one step further: he wears a white robe called a *kittel*. It's not actually a robe; it's a burial shroud. Traditional Jews wear it because, on Yom Kippur, we rehearse our own deaths, when our souls will be all that remains, along with the good works we do on earth. I stand in front of the Holy Ark, known as an *aron* in Hebrew. *Aron* is also the word for coffin. Shrouds have no pockets; "it all goes back in the box."

All of this is designed for one purpose: to encourage a serious personal accounting of the soul, a *cheshbon ha-nefesh,* an accounting that leads to transformation, to change, to renewal.

This renewal begins with the prayer called *Kol Nidrei,* a prayer for self-forgiveness. I get to start over, begin a new year with a clean slate.

The haunting melody, the words of the prayer, and the anticipation of the day ahead all combine to create a moment of high spiritual awareness—an awareness that, although the soul is housed in a body that is fallible, the soul itself is a spark of God. On Yom Kippur, the soul is freed—from guilt, blame, and fear—it is freed to be a reflection of godliness.

This renewal of spirit begins with forgiving oneself. I wanted to lose weight, but I didn't. I wanted to spend more time with the family, but I didn't. I wanted to ask my brother for forgiveness, but I didn't. Sure, I'm disappointed in myself for not being "perfect," for not honoring my promises to myself and others, for not fulfilling my resolutions. Yet, it is a new year. Tomorrow truly is another day. And I can try again.

You are a reflection of God, and you have goodness within. You have the power to forgive—not only those you have wronged but also yourself. Forgiving yourself begins with facing yourself, recognizing that you did the best you could at the time based on what you knew then, accepting responsibility, apologizing with sincerity, correcting what you can, crying for what you cannot, feeling the pain—and starting again.

Don't Go to Your Grave Mad

It takes courage to ask for forgiveness.
It takes courage to forgive.
Forgive others.
Forgive yourself.
It is within your spark of divinity to do it.
Put it on your God's To-Do List.

God's To-Do List

 Forgive

91. Never go to bed angry with your loved ones. Never.

92. Forgive someone for being late.

93. Forgive a debt.

94. Forgive yourself; God has.

95. Think of someone you wronged. Call. Say you're sorry. Ask for forgiveness.

96. If someone who has wronged you reaches out for reconciliation, offer forgiveness.

97. Forgive your politicians for their mistakes.

98. Forgive your clergy; they are overwhelmed.

99. Once a year, ask everyone you know for forgiveness. Others may never tell you of the hurt you caused.

100. Forgive God. God forgives you.

_____

_____

_____

_____

_____

_____

_____

_____

_____

What's Next?

When Michael "Be Like Mike" Jordan became a world-famous basketball star, the Nike shoe company hired him as a spokesperson. The television commercial featured a superhuman athlete performing what appeared to be an impossible feat—Jordan taking off from the foul line, fifteen feet from the basket, rising high above the ten-foot-high rim, and dunking the ball. After watching a human being accomplish this incredible act, this three-word tagline appeared in print across the screen: "Just Do It."

It's time for you to just do it.

Look back at each of the ten God's To-Do Lists. If you thought of specific acts of goodness God would put on your own personal To-Do List, take the best of the To-Dos and write them in on the blank My God's To-Do List page below. Copy the page from the book, and put it someplace where you cannot miss seeing it every day. Write your name on the top line. Look at the list every day. More important, *do* the To-Dos on your God's To-Do List. When you do one of the acts of godliness, place a check mark next to it—not as a way to check it off your list, but as a reminder that you have the potential to be an angel, to make a difference in the world, every day.

Create. Bless. Rest. Call. Comfort. Care. Repair. Wrestle. Give. Forgive.

Everyone has gifts to give and things to do. The world will be a better place because you are in it. The question is: are you ready to do the To-Dos on your God's To-Do List? Are you ready to be an angel?

There is a famous story of an eighteenth-century Hasidic master, Zusya, who was found one day by his students, distraught and teary:

"Master," they cried, "what bothers you so? You look frightened."

"I had a vision," Zusya replied, "that when I reach the Heavenly Court the angels will ask me about my life."

"But, Master, you are a scholar who has taught us well. You are a modest man. What question could they ask you that frightens you so?"

Zusya looked to the heavens and said: "The angels will not ask me: 'Why weren't you like Moses, who led the Israelites out of slavery and into freedom?' I am not Moses. They will not ask me: 'Why weren't you like Joshua, who took the people into the Promised Land?' I am not Joshua."

"What will they ask you, then?" the students wondered.

"They will say: 'There was only one thing no power on heaven or earth could have prevented you from becoming. They will ask me: 'Why weren't you Zusya?'"

When you get to heaven, what will you answer when the angels ask: "Were you the best *you* you could be? Did you live up to your potential? Did you fulfill your role in making this world—your world—a place filled with God's presence? In God's grand design, each human being has a unique contribution to make, a special way to do God's work on earth. Each human being is a full partner with God in the ongoing work of creation.

It's all about doing.

At the climax of the Shema prayer, the primary statement of faith of the Jewish people, this is the call from God:

> *Then you will remember and do all My To-Dos (mitzvot)*
> *And you will be holy before your God.*
>
> NUMBERS 15:40

Just do it.

Three More Ways to Be an Angel and Do God's Work on Earth

> *Just as face answers face in a reflection in water, so should one person's heart answer another's.*
>
> PROVERBS 27:19

Martin Buber, a great twentieth-century philosopher, taught that all life is about meeting between people. It is in *relationship* that human beings are elevated from an "I-It" to an "I-Thou" existence. God never intended for humans to be alone.

You are not alone.

You are surrounded by other human beings—made in the image of God—who have the same potential as you to be God's partner, to live their purpose, to do God's work on earth.

But, you need to remind them. So ...

Don't walk on by when you see another.

Remember the philtrum, that little indentation under everyone's nose. We were all once touched by an angel, and it's our task to recapture our ability to be an angel.

Don't give a cold shoulder. Offer a warm heart.

Share this book.

Share your new understanding of our purpose.

Welcome someone to the Partnership.

Begin with these final three To-Dos:

101. Look at every human being you meet,
     Face-to-face,
     Eye-to-eye,
     Heart-to-heart.

102. Recognize everyone's spark of divinity,
     And ...

103. Smile!

Welcome, Angels!

In the Jewish tradition, the Sabbath dinner begins with the singing of a hymn of hospitality, *Shalom Aleichem*, literally, "Welcome to You." The prayer welcomes God's "ministering" angels—those angels who serve God by serving God's people—into the home. Since it is traditional to invite guests to celebrate the Sabbath on Friday evening, the prayer also acts as a welcoming song for them.

The hymn's words are instructive. First, the angels are welcomed. Then, they are invited in. The angels have the power to bless and they are asked for a blessing. Finally, they are sent back out into the world, to bring their service and blessing to others.

This is my prayer for you. I welcome you as an angel and invite you into the worldwide community of God's angels of service who are dedicated to doing God's work on earth; I encourage you to see your work as a blessing— to others and to God. I send you out into the world to do your To-Dos, confident that you matter, that you can make a difference, that you are a blessing.

God bless you!

> *Welcome to you, ministering angels,*
> *Angels of the Most High,*
> *From the Ruler,*
> *The Ruler of Rulers,*
> *The Holy One, Praised is God.*
>
> *Come in peace,*
> *Angels of peace,*
> *Angels of the Most High,*
> *From the Ruler,*
> *The Ruler of Rulers,*
> *The Holy One, Praised is God.*
>
> *Bless me with peace,*
> *Angels of peace,*
> *Angels of the Most High,*
> *From the Ruler,*
> *The Ruler of Rulers,*
> *The Holy One, Praised is God.*

Go in peace,
Angels of peace,
Angels of the Most High,
From the Ruler,
The Ruler of Rulers,
The Holy One, Praised is God.

My God's To-Do List

✓ 1. Create

_____

✓ 2. Bless

_____

✓ 3. Rest

_____

✓ 4. Call

_____

✓ 5. Comfort

_____

✓ 6. Care

_____

✓ 7. Repair

_____

✓ 8. Wrestle

_____

✓ 9. Give

_____

✓ 10. Forgive

_____

God's To-Do List: Ten Days of Renewal

You may be invited to read this book as part of a congregational campaign called "God's To-Do List: Ten Days of Renewal." This is an opportunity for you to join with others in reading the book at the same time and hearing sermons about it from your spiritual leaders, with the goal of creating your personal God's To-Do List. You may also be invited to join small groups within your congregation for discussion and action.

For the Jewish reader, beginning on the Jewish New Year, you will join fellow congregants in reading *God's To-Do List* one chapter a day during the Ten Days of Renewal between Rosh Hashanah and Yom Kippur.

The Ten Days of Renewal are considered a time for personal reflection and spiritual renewal. Commonly known as the Ten Days of Awe or the Ten Days of Return, it is a period that begins with the prayers of Rosh Hashanah, celebrating the creation of the world—recognizing God's sovereignty, remembering God's covenant, and proclaiming God's majesty—and concludes with the prayers of Yom Kippur, the Day of Atonement, asking God and our fellow human beings to forgive our mistakes.

These Ten Days of Renewal are a wonderful opportunity to think about how you can do God's work on earth. By reading the book on the same schedule as others in the congregation, you may find yourself talking with family members, friends, and neighbors about how you can live your purpose as God's partner. Your rabbi may choose to talk about the themes in the book during High Holy Day sermons. Your congregation may offer a *God's To-Do List* discussion group during the Yom Kippur afternoon break. By the end of the Ten Days of Renewal, you will be ready to create your personal God's To-Do List to guide your efforts in the coming year. Your congregation may invite you to join a small group organized around important ways to be God's partner in repairing the world.

Here is a suggested schedule for reading *God's To-Do List* during the Ten Days of Renewal:

Day	Chapter to Read
1 Rosh Hashanah—First Day	Introduction/Create
2 Rosh Hashanah—Second Day	Bless
3	Rest
4	Call
5	Comfort
6	Care
7	Repair
8	Wrestle
9	Give
10 Yom Kippur	Forgive

Immediately after the break-fast of Yom Kippur, while your thoughts and ideas are still fresh, complete the My God's To-Do List at the end of the book.

For the Christian reader, your congregation may offer a God's To-Do List campaign spread over two weeks:

Day	Chapter to Read
Sunday	Introduction—Introductory Sermon "God's To-Do List"
Monday	Create
Tuesday	Bless
Wednesday	Rest
Thursday	Call
Friday	Comfort
Saturday	Care
Sunday	Repair—Sermon on "Repairing the World"
Monday	Wrestle
Tuesday	Give
Wednesday	Forgive
Thursday–Saturday	Writing My God's To-Do List
Sunday	Concluding Sermon—"Be an Angel" and God's To-Do List Sharing

Your congregation may also offer small groups, organized around specific ways to be an angel and do God's work on earth. Check out the God's To-Do List website, www.godstodolist.org, to see the lists of others, post your own, and read reports of God's angels doing God's work on earth.

Whatever your faith tradition, remember: every human being is made in the image of God. Keep your To-Do list someplace where you will see it every day. Do your list. Live your purpose. Be God's partner. And, remember, when you do ... you will be a blessing!

Sources Cited and Suggestions for Further Reading

Buber, Martin. *Tales of the Hasidim*. New York: Schocken Books, 1991.

Canfield, Jack, and Mark Victor Hansen. *Chicken Soup for the Soul: 101 Stories to Open the Heart & Rekindle the Spirit*. Deerfield Beach, FL: Health Communications, 1993.

Cohen, Norman. *Hineini in Our Lives: Learning How to Respond to Others through 14 Biblical Texts & Personal Stories*. Woodstock, VT: Jewish Lights, 2003.

Dorff, Elliot N. *The Way Into* Tikkun Olam *(Repairing the World)*. Woodstock, VT: Jewish Lights, 2005.

Eiseley, Loren. *The Unexpected Universe*. San Diego: Harcourt Brace Jovanovich, 1985.

Ford, Marcia. *The Sacred Art of Forgiveness: Forgiving Ourselves and Others through God's Grace*. Woodstock, VT: SkyLight Paths, 2006.

Fox, Everett. *The Five Books of Moses: Genesis, Exodus, Leviticus, Numbers, Deuteronomy*. New York: Schocken Books, 1995.

Gore, Al. *An Inconvenient Truth: The Planetary Emergency of Global Warming and What We Can Do about It*. Emmaus, PA: Rodale, 2006.

Heschel, Abraham Joshua. *The Sabbath: Its Meaning for Modern Man*. New York: Farrar, Straus and Giroux, 2005.

Kedar, Karyn D. *The Bridge to Forgiveness: Stories and Prayers for Finding God and Restoring Wholeness*. Woodstock, VT: Jewish Lights, 2007.

Kushner, Lawrence, and Gary Schmidt. *In God's Hands*. Woodstock, VT: Jewish Lights, 2005.

Lieber, David L. *Etz Hayim: Torah and Commentary*. Philadelphia: Jewish Publication Society, 2001.

Lipkis, Andy and Katie. *The Simple Act of Planting a Tree: A Citizen Forester's Guide to Healing Your Neighborhood, Your City, and Your World.* Los Angeles: J. P. Tarcher, 1990.

Ross, Dennis S. *God in Our Relationships: Spirituality between People from the Teachings of Martin Buber.* Woodstock, VT: Jewish Lights, 2003.

Schulweis, Harold. "Forgiveness and Reconciliation." Rosh Hashanah Sermon, 2000. www.vbs.org.

Schwarz, Sidney. *Judaism and Justice: The Jewish Passion to Repair the World.* Woodstock, VT: Jewish Lights, 2006.

Shapiro, Rami. *Ethics of the Sages:* Pirke Avot—*Annotated and Explained.* Woodstock, VT: SkyLight Paths, 2006.

———. *The Sacred Art of Lovingkindness: Preparing to Practice.* Woodstock, VT: SkyLight Paths, 2006.

Siegel, Danny. *Giving Your Money Away.* Pittsboro, NC: The Town House Press, 2006.

Warren, Rick. *The Purpose-Driven Life.* Grand Rapids, MI: Zondervan, 2002.

Wolfson, Ron. *Shabbat, 2nd Edition: The Family Guide to Preparing for and Celebrating the Sabbath.* Woodstock, VT: Jewish Lights, 2002.

———. *The Spirituality of Welcoming: How to Transform Your Congregation into a Sacred Community.* Woodstock, VT: Jewish Lights, 2006.

———. *A Time to Mourn, a Time to Comfort, 2nd Edition: A Guide to Jewish Bereavement.* Woodstock, VT: Jewish Lights, 2005.

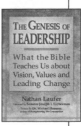

Congregation Resources

The Art of Public Prayer, 2nd Edition: Not for Clergy Only *By Lawrence A. Hoffman*
6 x 9, 272 pp, Quality PB, 978-1-893361-06-5 **$19.99** *(A SkyLight Paths book)*

Becoming a Congregation of Learners: Learning as a Key to Revitalizing
Congregational Life *By Isa Aron, PhD; Foreword by Rabbi Lawrence A. Hoffman*
6 x 9, 304 pp, Quality PB, 978-1-58023-089-6 **$19.95**

Finding a Spiritual Home: How a New Generation of Jews Can Transform the
American Synagogue *By Rabbi Sidney Schwarz*
6 x 9, 352 pp, Quality PB, 978-1-58023-185-5 **$19.95**

Jewish Pastoral Care, 2nd Edition: A Practical Handbook from Traditional &
Contemporary Sources *Edited by Rabbi Dayle A. Friedman*
6 x 9, 528 pp, HC, 978-1-58023-221-0 **$40.00**

Jewish Spiritual Direction: An Innovative Guide from Traditional and Contemporary
Sources *Edited by Rabbi Howard A. Addison and Barbara Eve Breitman*
6 x 9, 368 pp, HC, 978-1-58023-230-2 **$30.00**

The Self-Renewing Congregation: Organizational Strategies for Revitalizing
Congregational Life *By Isa Aron, PhD; Foreword by Dr. Ron Wolfson*
6 x 9, 304 pp, Quality PB, 978-1-58023-166-4 **$19.95**

Spiritual Community: The Power to Restore Hope, Commitment and Joy
By Rabbi David A. Teutsch, PhD 5½ x 8½, 144 pp, HC, 978-1-58023-270-8 **$19.99**

The Spirituality of Welcoming: How to Transform Your Congregation into a
Sacred Community *By Dr. Ron Wolfson* 6 x 9, 224 pp, Quality PB, 978-1-58023-244-9 **$19.99**

Rethinking Synagogues: A New Vocabulary for Congregational Life
By Rabbi Lawrence A. Hoffman 6 x 9, 240 pp, Quality PB, 978-1-58023-248-7 **$19.99**

Children's Books

What You Will See Inside a Synagogue
By Rabbi Lawrence A. Hoffman and Dr. Ron Wolfson; Full-color photos by Bill Aron
A colorful, fun-to-read introduction that explains the ways and whys of Jewish
worship and religious life.
8½ x 10½, 32 pp, Full-color photos, HC, 978-1-59473-012-2 **$17.99** *For ages 6 & up* *(A SkyLight Paths book)*

The Kids' Fun Book of Jewish Time
By Emily Sper 9 x 7½, 24 pp, Full-color illus., HC, 978-1-58023-311-8 **$16.99**

In God's Hands
By Lawrence Kushner and Gary Schmidt 9 x 12, 32 pp, HC, 978-1-58023-224-1 **$16.99**

Because Nothing Looks Like God
By Lawrence and Karen Kushner
Introduces children to the possibilities of spiritual life.
11 x 8½, 32 pp, Full-color illus., HC, 978-1-58023-092-6 **$16.95** *For ages 4 & up*

Also Available: **Because Nothing Looks Like God Teacher's Guide**
8½ x 11, 22 pp, PB, 978-1-58023-140-4 **$6.95** *For ages 5–8*
      Board Book Companions to *Because Nothing Looks Like God*
5 x 5, 24 pp, Full-color illus., SkyLight Paths Board Books *For ages 0–4*

What Does God Look Like? 978-1-893361-23-2 **$7.99**
How Does God Make Things Happen? 978-1-893361-24-9 **$7.95**
Where Is God? 978-1-893361-17-1 **$7.99**

The Book of Miracles: A Young Person's Guide to Jewish Spiritual Awareness
By Lawrence Kushner. All-new illustrations by the author
6 x 9, 96 pp, 2-color illus., HC, 978-1-879045-78-1 **$16.95** *For ages 9 and up*

In Our Image: God's First Creatures
By Nancy Sohn Swartz 9 x 12, 32 pp, Full-color illus., HC, 978-1-879045-99-6 **$16.95** *For ages 4 & up*

Also Available as a Board Book: **How Did the Animals Help God?**
5 x 5, 24 pp, Board, Full-color illus., 978-1-59473-044-3 **$7.99** *For ages 0–4* *(A SkyLight Paths book)*

What Makes Someone a Jew?
By Lauren Seidman
Reflects the changing face of American Judaism.
10 x 8½, 32 pp, Full-color photos, Quality PB Original, 978-1-58023-321-7 **$8.99** *For ages 3–6*

Current Events/History

The Story of the Jews: A 4,000-Year Adventure—A Graphic History Book
Written & illustrated by Stan Mack
Witty, illustrated narrative of all the major happenings from biblical times to the
twenty-first century. 6 x 9, 288 pp, illus., Quality PB, 978-1-58023-155-8 **$16.95**

Hannah Senesh: Her Life and Diary, the First Complete Edition
By Hannah Senesh; Foreword by Marge Piercy; Preface by Eitan Senesh
6 x 9, 352 pp, HC, 978-1-58023-212-8 **$24.99**

The Jewish Prophet: Visionary Words from Moses and Miriam to Henrietta Szold
and A. J. Heschel *By Rabbi Dr. Michael J. Shire*
6½ x 8½, 128 pp, 123 full-color illus., HC, 978-1-58023-168-8
Special gift price $14.95

Foundations of Sephardic Spirituality: The Inner Life of Jews of the Ottoman Empire
By Rabbi Marc D. Angel, PhD 6 x 9, 224 pp, HC, 978-1-58023-243-2 **$24.99**

Judaism and Justice: The Jewish Passion to Repair the World
By Rabbi Sidney Schwarz
6 x 9, 250 pp, HC, 978-1-58023-312-5 **$24.99**

Ecology

Ecology & the Jewish Spirit: Where Nature & the Sacred Meet
Edited by Ellen Bernstein 6 x 9, 288 pp, Quality PB, 978-1-58023-082-7 **$16.95**

Torah of the Earth: Exploring 4,000 Years of Ecology in Jewish Thought
Vol. 1: Biblical Israel: One Land, One People; Rabbinic Judaism: One People, Many Lands
Vol. 2: Zionism: One Land, Two Peoples; Eco-Judaism: One Earth, Many Peoples
Edited by Arthur Waskow
Vol. 1: 6 x 9, 272 pp, Quality PB, 978-1-58023-086-5 **$19.95**
Vol. 2: 6 x 9, 336 pp, Quality PB, 978-1-58023-087-2 **$19.95**

The Way Into Judaism and the Environment
By Jeremy Benstein 6 x 9, 224 pp, HC, 978-1-58023-268-5 **$24.99**

Grief/Healing

Against the Dying of the Light: A Parent's Story of Love, Loss and Hope
By Leonard Fein
5½ x 8½, 176 pp, Quality PB, 978-1-58023-197-8 **$15.99**

Grief in Our Seasons: A Mourner's Kaddish Companion *By Rabbi Kerry M. Olitzky*
4½ x 6½, 448 pp, Quality PB, 978-1-879045-55-2 **$15.95**

Healing of Soul, Healing of Body: Spiritual Leaders Unfold the Strength & Solace
in Psalms *Edited by Rabbi Simkha Y. Weintraub, CSW*
6 x 9, 128 pp, 2-color illus. text, Quality PB, 978-1-879045-31-6 **$14.99**

Jewish Paths toward Healing and Wholeness: A Personal Guide to Dealing with
Suffering *By Rabbi Kerry M. Olitzky; Foreword by Debbie Friedman.*
6 x 9, 192 pp, Quality PB, 978-1-58023-068-1 **$15.95**

Mourning & Mitzvah, 2nd Edition: A Guided Journal for Walking the Mourner's
Path through Grief to Healing *By Anne Brener, LCSW*
7½ x 9, 304 pp, Quality PB, 978-1-58023-113-8 **$19.99**

The Perfect Stranger's Guide to Funerals and Grieving Practices
A Guide to Etiquette in Other People's Religious Ceremonies *Edited by Stuart M. Matlins*
6 x 9, 240 pp, Quality PB, 978-1-893361-20-1 **$16.95** *(A SkyLight Paths book)*

Tears of Sorrow, Seeds of Hope, 2nd Edition: A Jewish Spiritual Companion for
Infertility and Pregnancy Loss *By Rabbi Nina Beth Cardin*
6 x 9, 208 pp, Quality PB, 978-1-58023-233-3 **$18.99**

A Time to Mourn, A Time to Comfort, 2nd Edition: A Guide to Jewish
Bereavement *By Dr. Ron Wolfson*
7 x 9, 384 pp, Quality PB, 978-1-58023-253-1 **$19.99**

When a Grandparent Dies: A Kid's Own Remembering Workbook for Dealing
with Shiva and the Year Beyond *By Nechama Liss-Levinson, PhD*
8 x 10, 48 pp, 2-color text, HC, 978-1-879045-44-6 **$15.95** *For ages 7–13*

Children's Books
by Sandy Eisenberg Sasso

Adam & Eve's First Sunset: God's New Day
Engaging new story explores fear and hope, faith and gratitude in ways that will delight kids and adults—inspiring us to bless each of God's days and nights.
9 x 12, 32 pp, Full-color illus., HC, 978-1-58023-177-0 **$17.95** *For ages 4 & up*

Also Available as a Board Book: **Adam and Eve's New Day**
5 x 5, 24 pp, Full-color illus., Board, 978-1-59473-205-8 **$7.99** *For ages 0–4 (A SkyLight Paths book)*

But God Remembered
Stories of Women from Creation to the Promised Land
Four different stories of women—Lillith, Serach, Bityah, and the Daughters of Z—teach us important values through their faith and actions.
9 x 12, 32 pp, Full-color illus., HC, 978-1-879045-43-9 **$16.95** *For ages 8 & up*

Cain & Abel: Finding the Fruits of Peace
Shows children that we have the power to deal with anger in positive ways. Provides questions for kids and adults to explore together.
9 x 12, 32 pp, Full-color illus., HC, 978-1-58023-123-7 **$16.95** *For ages 5 & up*

God in Between
If you wanted to find God, where would you look? This magical, mythical tale teaches that God can be found where we are: within all of us and the relationships between us.
9 x 12, 32 pp, Full-color illus., HC, 978-1-879045-86-6 **$16.95** *For ages 4 & up*

God's Paintbrush: Special 10th Anniversary Edition
Wonderfully interactive, invites children of all faiths and backgrounds to encounter God through moments in their own lives. Provides questions adult and child can explore together.
11 x 8½, 32 pp, Full-color illus., HC, 978-1-58023-195-4 **$17.95** *For ages 4 & up*

Also Available: **God's Paintbrush Teacher's Guide**
8½ x 11, 32 pp, PB, 978-1-879045-57-6 **$8.95**

God's Paintbrush Celebration Kit
A Spiritual Activity Kit for Teachers and Students of All Faiths, All Backgrounds
Additional activity sheets available:
8-Student Activity Sheet Pack (40 sheets/5 sessions), 978-1-58023-058-2 **$19.95**
Single-Student Activity Sheet Pack (5 sessions), 978-1-58023-059-9 **$3.95**

In God's Name
Like an ancient myth in its poetic text and vibrant illustrations, this award-winning modern fable about the search for God's name celebrates the diversity and, at the same time, the unity of all people.
9 x 12, 32 pp, Full-color illus., HC, 978-1-879045-26-2 **$16.99** *For ages 4 & up*

Also Available as a Board Book: **What Is God's Name?**
5 x 5, 24 pp, Board, Full-color illus., 978-1-893361-10-2 **$7.99** *For ages 0–4 (A SkyLight Paths book)*

Also Available: **In God's Name video and study guide**
Computer animation, original music, and children's voices. 18 min. **$29.99**

Also Available in Spanish: **El nombre de Dios**
9 x 12, 32 pp, Full-color illus., HC, 978-1-893361-63-8 **$16.95** *(A SkyLight Paths book)*

Noah's Wife: The Story of Naamah
When God tells Noah to bring the animals of the world onto the ark, God also calls on Naamah, Noah's wife, to save each plant on Earth. Based on an ancient text.
9 x 12, 32 pp, Full-color illus., HC, 978-1-58023-134-3 **$16.95** *For ages 4 & up*

Also Available as a Board Book: **Naamah, Noah's Wife**
5 x 5, 24 pp, Full-color illus., Board, 978-1-893361-56-0 **$7.95** *For ages 0–4 (A SkyLight Paths book)*

For Heaven's Sake: Finding God in Unexpected Places
9 x 12, 32 pp, Full-color illus., HC, 978-1-58023-054-4 **$16.95** *For ages 4 & up*

God Said Amen: Finding the Answers to Our Prayers
9 x 12, 32 pp, Full-color illus., HC, 978-1-58023-080-3 **$16.95** *For ages 4 & up*

Meditation

The Handbook of Jewish Meditation Practices
A Guide for Enriching the Sabbath and Other Days of Your Life
By Rabbi David A. Cooper Easy-to-learn meditation techniques.
6 x 9, 208 pp, Quality PB, 978-1-58023-102-2 **$16.95**

Discovering Jewish Meditation: Instruction & Guidance for Learning an Ancient
Spiritual Practice *By Nan Fink Gefen*
6 x 9, 208 pp, Quality PB, 978-1-58023-067-4 **$16.95**

A Heart of Stillness: A Complete Guide to Learning the Art of Meditation
By David A. Cooper 5½ x 8½, 272 pp, Quality PB, 978-1-893361-03-4 **$16.95** *(A SkyLight Paths book)*

Meditation from the Heart of Judaism: Today's Teachers Share Their
Practices, Techniques, and Faith *Edited by Avram Davis*
6 x 9, 256 pp, Quality PB, 978-1-58023-049-0 **$16.95**

Silence, Simplicity & Solitude: A Complete Guide to Spiritual Retreat at Home
By David A. Cooper 5½ x 8½, 336 pp, Quality PB, 978-1-893361-04-1 **$16.95**
(A SkyLight Paths book)

The Way of Flame: A Guide to the Forgotten Mystical Tradition of Jewish
Meditation *By Avram Davis* 4½ x 8, 176 pp, Quality PB, 978-1-58023-060-5 **$15.95**

Ritual/Sacred Practice/Journaling

The Jewish Dream Book: The Key to Opening the Inner Meaning of
Your Dreams *By Vanessa L. Ochs with Elizabeth Ochs; Full-color illus. by Kristina Swarner*
Instructions for how modern people can perform ancient Jewish dream practices
and dream interpretations drawn from the Jewish wisdom tradition.
8 x 8, 128 pp, Full-color illus., Deluxe PB w/flaps, 978-1-58023-132-9 **$16.95**

The Jewish Journaling Book: How to Use Jewish Tradition to Write
Your Life & Explore Your Soul *By Janet Ruth Falon*
Details the history of Jewish journaling throughout biblical and modern times, and
teaches specific journaling techniques to help you create and maintain a vital journal,
from a Jewish perspective. 8 x 8, 304 pp, Deluxe PB w/flaps, 978-1-58023-203-6 **$18.99**

The Book of Jewish Sacred Practices: CLAL's Guide to Everyday & Holiday
Rituals & Blessings *Edited by Rabbi Irwin Kula and Vanessa L. Ochs, PhD*
6 x 9, 368 pp, Quality PB, 978-1-58023-152-7 **$18.95**

Jewish Ritual: A Brief Introduction for Christians
By Rabbi Kerry M. Olitzky and Rabbi Daniel Judson
5½ x 8½, 144 pp, Quality PB, 978-1-58023-210-4 **$14.99**

The Rituals & Practices of a Jewish Life: A Handbook for Personal Spiritual
Renewal *Edited by Rabbi Kerry M. Olitzky and Rabbi Daniel Judson*
6 x 9, 272 pp, illus., Quality PB, 978-1-58023-169-5 **$18.95**

The Sacred Art of Lovingkindness: Preparing to Practice
By Rabbi Rami Shapiro 5½ x 8½, 176 pp, Quality PB, 978-1-59473-151-8 **$16.99**
(A SkyLight Paths book)

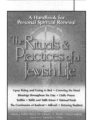

Science Fiction/Mystery & Detective Fiction

Mystery Midrash: An Anthology of Jewish Mystery & Detective Fiction
Edited by Lawrence W. Raphael; Preface by Joel Siegel
6 x 9, 304 pp, Quality PB, 978-1-58023-055-1 **$16.95**

Criminal Kabbalah: An Intriguing Anthology of Jewish Mystery & Detective Fiction
Edited by Lawrence W. Raphael; Foreword by Laurie R. King
6 x 9, 256 pp, Quality PB, 978-1-58023-109-1 **$16.95**

Wandering Stars: An Anthology of Jewish Fantasy & Science Fiction
Edited by Jack Dann; Introduction by Isaac Asimov
6 x 9, 272 pp, Quality PB, 978-1-58023-005-6 **$16.95**

More Wandering Stars: An Anthology of Outstanding Stories of Jewish Fantasy and
Science Fiction *Edited by Jack Dann; Introduction by Isaac Asimov*
6 x 9, 192 pp, Quality PB, 978-1-58023-063-6 **$16.95**

Holidays/Holy Days

Rosh Hashanah Readings: Inspiration, Information and Contemplation
Yom Kippur Readings: Inspiration, Information and Contemplation
Edited by Rabbi Dov Peretz Elkins with Section Introductions from Arthur Green's These Are the Words
An extraordinary collection of readings, prayers and insights that enable the modern worshiper to enter into the spirit of the High Holy Days in a personal and powerful way, permitting the meaning of the Jewish New Year to enter the heart.
RHR: 6 x 9, 400 pp, HC, 978-1-58023-239-5 **$24.99**
YKR: 6 x 9, 368 pp, HC, 978-1-58023-271-5 **$24.99**

Jewish Holidays: A Brief Introduction for Christians
By Rabbi Kerry M. Olitzky and Rabbi Daniel Judson
5½ x 8½, 144 pp, Quality PB, 978-1-58023-302-6 **$16.99**

Leading the Passover Journey: The Seder's Meaning Revealed, the Haggadah's Story Retold   *By Rabbi Nathan Laufer*
Uncovers the hidden meaning of the Seder's rituals and customs.
6 x 9, 224 pp, HC, 978-1-58023-211-1 **$24.99**

Reclaiming Judaism as a Spiritual Practice: Holy Days and Shabbat
By Rabbi Goldie Milgram
7 x 9, 272 pp, Quality PB, 978-1-58023-205-0 **$19.99**

7th Heaven: Celebrating Shabbat with Rebbe Nachman of Breslov
By Moshe Mykoff with the Breslov Research Institute
5⅛ x 8¼, 224 pp, Deluxe PB w/flaps, 978-1-58023-175-6 **$18.95**

The Women's Passover Companion: Women's Reflections on the Festival of Freedom   *Edited by Rabbi Sharon Cohen Anisfeld, Tara Mohr, and Catherine Spector*
Groundbreaking. A provocative conversation about women's relationships to Passover as well as the roots and meanings of women's seders.
6 x 9, 352 pp, Quality PB, 978-1-58023-231-9 **$19.99**

The Women's Seder Sourcebook: Rituals & Readings for Use at the Passover Seder   *Edited by Rabbi Sharon Cohen Anisfeld, Tara Mohr, and Catherine Spector*
Gathers the voices of more than one hundred women in readings, personal and creative reflections, commentaries, blessings, and ritual suggestions that can be incorporated into your Passover celebration.
6 x 9, 384 pp, Quality PB, 978-1-58023-232-6 **$19.99**

Creating Lively Passover Seders: A Sourcebook of Engaging Tales, Texts & Activities
By David Arnow, PhD   7 x 9, 416 pp, Quality PB, 978-1-58023-184-8 **$24.99**

Hanukkah, 2nd Edition: The Family Guide to Spiritual Celebration
By Dr. Ron Wolfson. Edited by Joel Lurie Grishaver.
7 x 9, 240 pp, illus., Quality PB, 978-1-58023-122-0 **$18.95**

The Jewish Family Fun Book: Holiday Projects, Everyday Activities, and Travel Ideas
with Jewish Themes   *By Danielle Dardashti and Roni Sarig. Illus. by Avi Katz.*
6 x 9, 288 pp, 70+ b/w illus. & diagrams, Quality PB, 978-1-58023-171-8 **$18.95**

The Jewish Gardening Cookbook: Growing Plants & Cooking for Holidays
& Festivals   *By Michael Brown*   6 x 9, 224 pp, 30+ b/w illus., Quality PB, 978-1-58023-116-9 **$16.95**

The Jewish Lights Book of Fun Classroom Activities: Simple and Seasonal
Projects for Teachers and Students   *By Danielle Dardashti and Roni Sarig*
6 x 9, 240 pp, Quality PB, 978-1-58023-206-7 **$19.99**

Passover, 2nd Edition: The Family Guide to Spiritual Celebration
By Dr. Ron Wolfson with Joel Lurie Grishaver   7 x 9, 352 pp, Quality PB, 978-1-58023-174-9 **$19.95**

Shabbat, 2nd Edition: The Family Guide to Preparing for and Celebrating the Sabbath
By Dr. Ron Wolfson   7 x 9, 320 pp, illus., Quality PB, 978-1-58023-164-0 **$19.99**

Sharing Blessings: Children's Stories for Exploring the Spirit of the Jewish Holidays
By Rahel Musleah and Rabbi Michael Klayman
8½ x 11, 64 pp, Full-color illus., HC, 978-1-879045-71-2 **$18.95** *For ages 6 & up*

Life Cycle
Marriage / Parenting / Family / Aging

Jewish Fathers: A Legacy of Love
Photographs by Lloyd Wolf. Essays by Paula Wolfson. Foreword by Rabbi Harold Kushner.
Honors the role of contemporary Jewish fathers in America. Each father tells in his own words what it means to be a parent and Jewish, and what he learned from his own father. Insightful photos.
10¾ x 9⅞, 144 pp with 100+ duotone photos, HC, 978-1-58023-204-3 **$30.00**

The New Jewish Baby Album: Creating and Celebrating the Beginning of a Spiritual Life—A Jewish Lights Companion
By the Editors at Jewish Lights. Foreword by Anita Diamant. Preface by Rabbi Sandy Eisenberg Sasso.
A spiritual keepsake that will be treasured for generations. More than just a memory book, *shows you how—and why it's important*—to create a Jewish home and a Jewish life. 8 x 10, 64 pp, Deluxe Padded HC, Full-color illus., 978-1-58023-138-1 **$19.95**

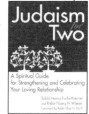

The Jewish Pregnancy Book: A Resource for the Soul, Body & Mind during Pregnancy, Birth & the First Three Months
By Sandy Falk, MD, and Rabbi Daniel Judson, with Steven A. Rapp
Includes medical information, prayers and rituals for each stage of pregnancy, from a liberal Jewish perspective. 7 x 10, 208 pp, Quality PB, b/w photos, 978-1-58023-178-7 **$16.95**

Celebrating Your New Jewish Daughter: Creating Jewish Ways to Welcome Baby Girls into the Covenant—New and Traditional Ceremonies *By Debra Nussbaum Cohen; Foreword by Rabbi Sandy Eisenberg Sasso* 6 x 9, 272 pp, Quality PB, 978-1-58023-090-2 **$18.95**

The New Jewish Baby Book, 2nd Edition: Names, Ceremonies & Customs—A Guide for Today's Families *By Anita Diamant* 6 x 9, 336 pp, Quality PB, 978-1-58023-251-7 **$19.99**

Parenting As a Spiritual Journey: Deepening Ordinary and Extraordinary Events into Sacred Occasions *By Rabbi Nancy Fuchs-Kreimer*
6 x 9, 224 pp, Quality PB, 978-1-58023-016-2 **$16.95**

Parenting Jewish Teens: A Guide for the Perplexed
By Joanne Doades 6 x 9, 200 pp, Quality PB, 978-1-58023-305-7 **$16.99**

Judaism for Two: A Spiritual Guide for Strengthening and Celebrating Your Loving Relationship *By Rabbi Nancy Fuchs-Kreimer and Rabbi Nancy H. Wiener; Foreword by Rabbi Elliot N. Dorff* Addresses the ways Jewish teachings can enhance and strengthen committed relationships. 6 x 9, 224 pp, Quality PB, 978-1-58023-254-8 **$16.99**

Embracing the Covenant: Converts to Judaism Talk About Why & How
By Rabbi Allan Berkowitz and Patti Moskovitz 6 x 9, 192 pp, Quality PB, 978-1-879045-50-7 **$16.95**

The Guide to Jewish Interfaith Family Life: An InterfaithFamily.com Handbook
Edited by Ronnie Friedland and Edmund Case 6 x 9, 384 pp, Quality PB, 978-1-58023-153-4 **$18.95**

Introducing My Faith and My Community
The Jewish Outreach Institute Guide for the Christian in a Jewish Interfaith Relationship
By Rabbi Kerry M. Olitzky 6 x 9, 176 pp, Quality PB, 978-1-58023-192-3 **$16.99**

Making a Successful Jewish Interfaith Marriage: The Jewish Outreach Institute Guide to Opportunities, Challenges and Resources *By Rabbi Kerry M. Olitzky with Joan Peterson Littman*
6 x 9, 176 pp, Quality PB, 978-1-58023-170-1 **$16.95**

The Creative Jewish Wedding Book: A Hands-On Guide to New & Old
Traditions, Ceremonies & Celebrations *By Gabrielle Kaplan-Mayer*
9 x 9, 288 pp, b/w photos, Quality PB, 978-1-58023-194-7 **$19.99**

Divorce Is a Mitzvah: A Practical Guide to Finding Wholeness and Holiness When Your Marriage Dies *By Rabbi Perry Netter; Afterword by Rabbi Laura Geller.*
6 x 9, 224 pp, Quality PB, 978-1-58023-172-5 **$16.95**

A Heart of Wisdom: Making the Jewish Journey from Midlife through the Elder Years
Edited by Susan Berrin; Foreword by Harold Kushner
6 x 9, 384 pp, Quality PB, 978-1-58023-051-3 **$18.95**

So That Your Values Live On: Ethical Wills and How to Prepare Them
Edited by Jack Riemer and Nathaniel Stampfer
6 x 9, 272 pp, Quality PB, 978-1-879045-34-7 **$18.99**

Theology/Philosophy/The Way Into... Series

The Way Into... series offers an accessible and highly usable "guided tour" of the Jewish faith, people, history and beliefs—in total, an introduction to Judaism that will enable you to understand and interact with the sacred texts of the Jewish tradition. Each volume is written by a leading contemporary scholar and teacher, and explores one key aspect of Judaism. *The Way Into...* series enables all readers to achieve a real sense of Jewish cultural literacy through guided study.

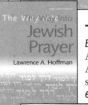

The Way Into Encountering God in Judaism
By Neil Gillman
For everyone who wants to understand how Jews have encountered God throughout history and today.
6 x 9, 240 pp, Quality PB, 978-1-58023-199-2 **$18.99**; HC, 978-1-58023-025-4 **$21.95**
Also Available: **The Jewish Approach to God:** A Brief Introduction for Christians
By Neil Gillman
5½ x 8½, 192 pp, Quality PB, 978-1-58023-190-9 **$16.95**

The Way Into Jewish Mystical Tradition
By Lawrence Kushner
Allows readers to interact directly with the sacred mystical text of the Jewish tradition. An accessible introduction to the concepts of Jewish mysticism, their religious and spiritual significance and how they relate to life today.
6 x 9, 224 pp, Quality PB, 978-1-58023-200-5 **$18.99**; HC, 978-1-58023-029-2 **$21.95**

The Way Into Jewish Prayer
By Lawrence A. Hoffman
Opens the door to 3,000 years of Jewish prayer, making available all anyone needs to feel at home in the Jewish way of communicating with God.
6 x 9, 208 pp, Quality PB, 978-1-58023-201-2 **$18.99**

The Way Into Judaism and the Environment
By Jeremy Benstein
Explores the ways in which Judaism contributes to contemporary social-environmental issues, the extent to which Judaism is part of the problem and how it can be part of the solution.
6 x 9, 288 pp, HC, 978-1-58023-268-5 **$24.99**

The Way Into *Tikkun Olam* (Repairing the World)
By Elliot N. Dorff
An accessible introduction to the Jewish concept of the individual's responsibility to care for others and repair the world.
6 x 9, 320 pp, HC, 978-1-58023-269-2 **$24.99**

The Way Into Torah
By Norman J. Cohen
Helps guide in the exploration of the origins and development of Torah, explains why it should be studied and how to do it.
6 x 9, 176 pp, Quality PB, 978-1-58023-198-5 **$16.99**; HC, 978-1-58023-028-5 **$21.95**

The Way Into the Varieties of Jewishness
By Sylvia Barack Fishman, PhD
Explores the religious and historical understanding of what it has meant to be Jewish from ancient times to the present controversy over "Who is a Jew?"
6 x 9, 288 pp, HC, 978-1-58023-030-8 **$24.99**

Theology/Philosophy

Christians and Jews in Dialogue: Learning in the Presence of the Other
By Mary C. Boys and Sara S. Lee; Foreword by Dr. Dorothy Bass
6 x 9, 240 pp, HC, 978-1-59473-144-0 **$21.99** *(A SkyLight Paths book)*

The Death of Death: Resurrection and Immortality in Jewish Thought
By Neil Gillman 6 x 9, 336 pp, Quality PB, 978-1-58023-081-0 **$18.95**

Ethics of the Sages: *Pirke Avot*—Annotated & Explained
Translation & Annotation by Rabbi Rami Shapiro
5½ x 8½, 208 pp, Quality PB, 978-1-59473-207-2 **$16.99** *(A SkyLight Paths book)*

Evolving Halakhah: A Progressive Approach to Traditional Jewish Law
By Rabbi Dr. Moshe Zemer 6 x 9, 480 pp, Quality PB, 978-1-58023-127-5 **$29.95**;
HC, 978-1-58023-002-5 **$40.00**

Hasidic Tales: Annotated & Explained
By Rabbi Rami Shapiro; Foreword by Andrew Harvey
5½ x 8½, 240 pp, Quality PB, 978-1-893361-86-7 **$16.95** *(A SkyLight Paths Book)*

Healing the Jewish-Christian Rift: Growing Beyond our Wounded History
By Ron Miller and Laura Bernstein; Foreword by Dr. Beatrice Bruteau
6 x 9, 288 pp, Quality PB, 978-1-59473-139-6 **$18.99** *(A SkyLight Paths book)*

A Heart of Many Rooms: Celebrating the Many Voices within Judaism
By David Hartman 6 x 9, 352 pp, Quality PB, 978-1-58023-156-5 **$19.95**

The Hebrew Prophets: Selections Annotated & Explained
Translation & Annotation by Rabbi Rami Shapiro; Foreword by Zalman M. Schachter-Shalomi
5½ x 8½, 224 pp, Quality PB, 978-1-59473-037-5 **$16.99** *(A SkyLight Paths book)*

A Jewish Understanding of the New Testament
By Rabbi Samuel Sandmel; Preface by Rabbi David Sandmel
5½ x 8½, 368 pp, Quality PB, 978-1-59473-048-1 **$19.99** *(A SkyLight Paths book)*

Keeping Faith with the Psalms: Deepen Your Relationship with God Using the Book
of Psalms *By Daniel F. Polish* 6 x 9, 320 pp, Quality PB, 978-1-58023-300-2 **$18.99**;
HC, 978-1-58023-179-4 **$24.95**

A Living Covenant: The Innovative Spirit in Traditional Judaism
By David Hartman 6 x 9, 368 pp, Quality PB, 978-1-58023-011-7 **$20.00**

Love and Terror in the God Encounter
The Theological Legacy of Rabbi Joseph B. Soloveitchik
By David Hartman 6 x 9, 240 pp, Quality PB, 978-1-58023-176-3 **$19.95**;
HC, 978-1-58023-112-1 **$25.00**

The Personhood of God: Biblical Theology, Human Faith and the Divine Image
By Dr. Yochanan Muffs; Foreword by Dr. David Hartman
6 x 9, 240 pp, HC, 978-1-58023-265-4 **$24.99**

Tormented Master: The Life and Spiritual Quest of Rabbi Nahman of Bratslav
By Arthur Green 6 x 9, 416 pp, Quality PB, 978-1-879045-11-8 **$19.99**

Traces of God: Seeing God in Torah, History and Everyday Life
By Neil Gillman 6 x 9, 240 pp, HC, 978-1-58023-249-4 **$21.99**

We Jews and Jesus: Exploring Theological Differences for Mutual Understanding
By Rabbi Samuel Sandmel; Preface by Rabbi David Sandmel
6 x 9, 176 pp, Quality PB, 978-1-59473-208-9 **$16.99** *(A SkyLight Paths book)*

Your Word Is Fire: The Hasidic Masters on Contemplative Prayer
Edited and translated by Arthur Green and Barry W. Holtz
6 x 9, 160 pp, Quality PB, 978-1-879045-25-5 **$15.95**

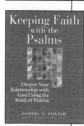

I Am Jewish
Personal Reflections Inspired by the Last Words of Daniel Pearl

Almost 150 Jews—both famous and not—from all walks of life, from all around
the world, write about Identity, Heritage, Covenant / Chosenness and Faith,
Humanity and Ethnicity, and *Tikkun Olam* and Justice.
Edited by Judea and Ruth Pearl
6 x 9, 304 pp, Deluxe PB w/flaps, 978-1-58023-259-3 **$18.99**; HC, 978-1-58023-183-1 **$24.99**
**Download a free copy of the *I Am Jewish Teacher's Guide* at our website:
www.jewishlights.com**

Spirituality

The Adventures of Rabbi Harvey: A Graphic Novel of Jewish Wisdom and Wit in the Wild West *By Steve Sheinkin*
Jewish and American folktales combine in this witty and original graphic novel collection. Creatively retold and set on the western frontier of the 1870s.
6 x 9, 144 pp, Full-color illus., Quality PB, 978-1-58023-310-1 **$16.99**
Also Available: **The Adventures of Rabbi Harvey Teacher's Guide**
8½ x 11, 32 pp, PB, 978-1-58023-326-2 **$8.99**

Ethics of the Sages: Pirke Avot—Annotated & Explained
Translation and Annotation by Rabbi Rami Shapiro
5½ x 8½, 192 pp, Quality PB, 978-1-59473-207-2 **$16.99** *(A SkyLight Paths book)*

A Book of Life: Embracing Judaism as a Spiritual Practice
By Michael Strassfeld 6 x 9, 528 pp, Quality PB, 978-1-58023-247-0 **$19.99**

Meaning and Mitzvah: Daily Practices for Reclaiming Judaism through Prayer, God, Torah, Hebrew, Mitzvot and Peoplehood *By Rabbi Goldie Milgram*
7 x 9, 336 pp, Quality PB, 978-1-58023-256-2 **$19.99**

The Soul of the Story: Meetings with Remarkable People
By Rabbi David Zeller 6 x 9, 288 pp, HC, 978-1-58023-272-2 **$21.99**

Aleph-Bet Yoga: Embodying the Hebrew Letters for Physical and Spiritual Well-Being
By Steven A. Rapp. Foreword by Tamar Frankiel, PhD and Judy Greenfeld. Preface by Hart Lazer.
7 x 10, 128 pp, b/w photos, Quality PB, Layflat binding, 978-1-58023-162-6 **$16.95**

Entering the Temple of Dreams: Jewish Prayers, Movements, and Meditations for the End of the Day *By Tamar Frankiel, PhD, and Judy Greenfeld*
7 x 10, 192 pp, illus., Quality PB, 978-1-58023-079-7 **$16.95**

Does the Soul Survive? A Jewish Journey to Belief in Afterlife, Past Lives & Living with Purpose *By Rabbi Elie Kaplan Spitz; Foreword by Brian L. Weiss, MD*
6 x 9, 288 pp, Quality PB, 978-1-58023-165-7 **$16.99**

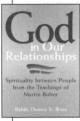

First Steps to a New Jewish Spirit: Reb Zalman's Guide to Recapturing the Intimacy & Ecstasy in Your Relationship with God *By Rabbi Zalman M. Schachter-Shalomi with Donald Gropman* 6 x 9, 144 pp, Quality PB, 978-1-58023-182-4 **$16.95**

God in Our Relationships: Spirituality between People from the Teachings of Martin Buber *By Rabbi Dennis S. Ross* 5½ x 8½, 160 pp, Quality PB, 978-1-58023-147-3 **$16.95**

Judaism, Physics and God: Searching for Sacred Metaphors in a Post-Einstein World
By Rabbi David W. Nelson 6 x 9, 368 pp, Quality PB, inc. reader's discussion guide, 978-1-58023-306-4 **$18.99**;
HC, 352 pp, 978-1-58023-252-4 **$24.99**

The Jewish Lights Spirituality Handbook: A Guide to Understanding, Exploring & Living a Spiritual Life *Edited by Stuart M. Matlins*
What exactly is "Jewish" about spirituality? How do I make it a part of my life? Fifty of today's foremost spiritual leaders share their ideas and experience with us.
6 x 9, 456 pp, Quality PB, 978-1-58023-093-3 **$19.99**

Bringing the Psalms to Life: How to Understand and Use the Book of Psalms
By Daniel F. Polish 6 x 9, 208 pp, Quality PB, 978-1-58023-157-2 **$16.95**;
HC, 978-1-58023-077-3 **$21.95**

God & the Big Bang: Discovering Harmony between Science & Spirituality
By Daniel C. Matt 6 x 9, 216 pp, Quality PB, 978-1-879045-89-7 **$16.99**

Minding the Temple of the Soul: Balancing Body, Mind, and Spirit through Traditional Jewish Prayer, Movement, and Meditation *By Tamar Frankiel, PhD, and Judy Greenfeld*
7 x 10, 184 pp, illus., Quality PB, 978-1-879045-64-4 **$16.95**
Audiotape of the Blessings and Meditations: 60 min. **$9.95**
Videotape of the Movements and Meditations: 46 min. **$20.00**

One God Clapping: The Spiritual Path of a Zen Rabbi *By Alan Lew with Sherril Jaffe*
5½ x 8½, 336 pp, Quality PB, 978-1-58023-115-2 **$16.95**

There Is No Messiah ... and You're It: The Stunning Transformation of Judaism's Most Provocative Idea *By Rabbi Robert N. Levine, DD*
6 x 9, 192 pp, Quality PB, 978-1-58023-255-5 **$16.99**

These Are the Words: A Vocabulary of Jewish Spiritual Life
By Arthur Green 6 x 9, 304 pp, Quality PB, 978-1-58023-107-7 **$18.95**

Spirituality/Lawrence Kushner

Filling Words with Light: Hasidic and Mystical Reflections on Jewish Prayer
By Lawrence Kushner and Nehemia Polen
5½ x 8½, 176 pp, HC, 978-1-58023-216-6 **$21.99**

The Book of Letters: A Mystical Hebrew Alphabet
Popular HC Edition, 6 x 9, 80 pp, 2-color text, 978-1-879045-00-2 **$24.95**
Collector's Limited Edition, 9 x 12, 80 pp, gold foil embossed pages, w/limited edition silkscreened print, 978-1-879045-04-0 **$349.00**

The Book of Miracles: A Young Person's Guide to Jewish Spiritual Awareness
6 x 9, 96 pp, 2-color illus., HC, 978-1-879045-78-1 **$16.95** *For ages 9 and up*

The Book of Words: Talking Spiritual Life, Living Spiritual Talk
6 x 9, 160 pp, Quality PB, 978-1-58023-020-9 **$16.95**

Eyes Remade for Wonder: A Lawrence Kushner Reader *Introduction by Thomas Moore*
6 x 9, 240 pp, Quality PB, 978-1-58023-042-1 **$18.95**

God Was in This Place & I, i Did Not Know: Finding Self, Spirituality and Ultimate Meaning   6 x 9, 192 pp, Quality PB, 978-1-879045-33-0 **$16.95**

Honey from the Rock: An Introduction to Jewish Mysticism
6 x 9, 176 pp, Quality PB, 978-1-58023-073-5 **$16.95**

Invisible Lines of Connection: Sacred Stories of the Ordinary
5½ x 8¼, 160 pp, Quality PB, 978-1-879045-98-9 **$15.95**

Jewish Spirituality—A Brief Introduction for Christians
5½ x 8¼, 112 pp, Quality PB, 978-1-58023-150-3 **$12.95**

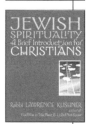

The River of Light: Jewish Mystical Awareness
6 x 9, 192 pp, Quality PB, 978-1-58023-096-4 **$16.95**

The Way Into Jewish Mystical Tradition
6 x 9, 224 pp, Quality PB, 978-1-58023-200-5 **$18.99**; HC, 978-1-58023-029-2 **$21.95**

Spirituality/Prayer

Pray Tell: A Hadassah Guide to Jewish Prayer
By Rabbi Jules Harlow, with contributions from many others
8½ x 11, 400 pp, Quality PB, 978-1-58023-163-3 **$29.95**

Witnesses to the One: The Spiritual History of the *Sh'ma* By Rabbi Joseph B. Meszler;
Foreword by Rabbi Elyse Goldstein 6 x 9, 176 pp, HC, 978-1-58023-309-5 **$19.99**

My People's Prayer Book Series

Traditional Prayers, Modern Commentaries   *Edited by Rabbi Lawrence A. Hoffman*
Provides diverse and exciting commentary to the traditional liturgy, helping modern men and women find new wisdom in Jewish prayer, and bring liturgy into their lives. Each book includes Hebrew text, modern translation, and commentaries from all perspectives of the Jewish world.

Vol. 1—The Sh'ma and Its Blessings
7 x 10, 168 pp, HC, 978-1-879045-79-8 **$24.99**

Vol. 2—The Amidah
7 x 10, 240 pp, HC, 978-1-879045-80-4 **$24.95**

Vol. 3—P'sukei D'zimrah (Morning Psalms)
7 x 10, 240 pp, HC, 978-1-879045-81-1 **$24.95**

Vol. 4—Seder K'riat Hatorah (The Torah Service)
7 x 10, 264 pp, HC, 978-1-879045-82-8 **$23.95**

Vol. 5—Birkhot Hashachar (Morning Blessings)
7 x 10, 240 pp, HC, 978-1-879045-83-5 **$24.95**

Vol. 6—Tachanun and Concluding Prayers
7 x 10, 240 pp, HC, 978-1-879045-84-2 **$24.95**

Vol. 7—Shabbat at Home
7 x 10, 240 pp, HC, 978-1-879045-85-9 **$24.95**

Vol. 8—Kabbalat Shabbat (Welcoming Shabbat in the Synagogue)
7 x 10, 240 pp, HC, 978-1-58023-121-3 **$24.99**

Vol. 9—Welcoming the Night: Minchah and Ma'ariv (Afternoon and Evening Prayer) 7 x 10, 272 pp, HC, 978-1-58023-262-3 **$24.99**

Vol. 10—Shabbat Morning: Shacharit and Musaf (Morning and Additional Services) 7 x 10, 240 pp, HC, 978-1-58023-240-1 **$24.99**

Pastoral Care Resources
LifeLights/™אורות החיים

LifeLights/™אורות החיים are inspirational, informational booklets about challenges to our emotional and spiritual lives and how to deal with them. Offering help for wholeness and healing, each LifeLight is written from a uniquely Jewish spiritual perspective by a wise and caring soul—someone who knows the inner territory of grief, doubt, confusion and longing.

In addition to providing wise words to light a difficult path, each LifeLight booklet provides suggestions for additional resources for reading. Many list organizations, Jewish and secular, that can provide help, along with information on how to contact them.

Categories/Sample Topics:

Health & Healing
Caring for Yourself/When Someone Is Ill
Facing Cancer as a Family
Recognizing a Loved One's Addiction, and Providing Help

Loss / Grief / Death & Dying
Coping with the Death of a Spouse
From Death through Shiva: A Guide to Jewish Grieving Practices
Taking the Time You Need to Mourn Your Loss
Talking to Children about Death

Judaism / Living a Jewish Life
Bar and Bat Mitzvah's Meaning: Preparing Spiritually with Your Child
Yearning for God

Family Issues
Grandparenting Interfaith Grandchildren
Talking to Your Children about God

Spiritual Care / Personal Growth
Easing the Burden of Stress
Finding a Way to Forgive
Praying in Hard Times

Now available in hundreds of congregations, health-care facilities, funeral homes, colleges and military installations, these helpful, comforting resources can be uniquely presented in LifeLights display racks, available from Jewish Lights. **Each LifeLight topic is sold in packs of twelve for $9.95.** General discounts are available for quantity purchases.

Visit us online at **www.jewishlights.com** for a complete list of titles, authors, prices and ordering information, or call us at (802) 457-4000 or toll free at (800) 962-4544.

I Am Jewish
Personal Reflections Inspired by the Last Words of Daniel Pearl

Almost 150 Jews—both famous and not—from all walks of life, from all around the world, write about Identity, Heritage, Covenant / Chosenness and Faith, Humanity and Ethnicity, and *Tikkun Olam* and Justice.

Edited by Judea and Ruth Pearl
6 x 9, 304 pp, Deluxe PB w/flaps, 978-1-58023-259-3 **$18.99**; HC, 978-1-58023-183-1 **$24.99**
Download a free copy of the *I Am Jewish Teacher's Guide* at our website:
www.jewishlights.com

Spirituality/Women's Interest

The Quotable Jewish Woman: Wisdom, Inspiration & Humor from the Mind & Heart
Edited and compiled by Elaine Bernstein Partnow
6 x 9, 496 pp, HC, 978-1-58023-193-0 **$29.99**

The Knitting Way: A Guide to Spiritual Self-Discovery *By Linda Skolnick and Janice MacDaniels* 7 x 9, 240 pp, Quality PB, 978-1-59473-079-5 **$16.99** *(A SkyLight Paths book)*

The Quilting Path: A Guide to Spiritual Self-Discovery through Fabric, Thread and Kabbalah
By Louise Silk 7 x 9, 192 pp, Quality PB, 978-1-59473-206-5 **$16.99** *(A SkyLight Paths book)*

The Divine Feminine in Biblical Wisdom Literature: Selections Annotated & Explained *Translated and Annotated by Rabbi Rami Shapiro*
5½ x 8½, 240 pp, Quality PB, 978-1-59473-109-9 **$16.99** *(A SkyLight Paths book)*

Lifecycles, Vol. 1: Jewish Women on Life Passages & Personal Milestones
Edited and with Introductions by Rabbi Debra Orenstein
6 x 9, 480 pp, Quality PB, 978-1-58023-018-6 **$19.95**

Lifecycles, Vol. 2: Jewish Women on Biblical Themes in Contemporary Life
Edited and with Introductions by Rabbi Debra Orenstein and Rabbi Jane Rachel Litman
6 x 9, 464 pp, Quality PB, 978-1-58023-019-3 **$19.95**

Moonbeams: A Hadassah Rosh Hodesh Guide *Edited by Carol Diament, PhD*
8½ x 11, 240 pp, Quality PB, 978-1-58023-099-5 **$20.00**

ReVisions: Seeing Torah through a Feminist Lens *By Rabbi Elyse Goldstein*
5½ x 8½, 224 pp, Quality PB, 978-1-58023-117-6 **$16.95**

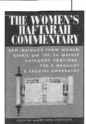

The Women's Haftarah Commentary: New Insights from Women Rabbis on the 54 Weekly Haftarah Portions, the 5 Megillot & Special Shabbatot
Edited by Rabbi Elyse Goldstein 6 x 9, 560 pp, HC, 978-1-58023-133-6 **$39.99**

The Women's Torah Commentary: New Insights from Women Rabbis on the 54 Weekly Torah Portions *Edited by Rabbi Elyse Goldstein*
6 x 9, 496 pp, HC, 978-1-58023-076-6 **$34.95**

The Year Mom Got Religion: One Woman's Midlife Journey into Judaism
By Lee Meyerhoff Hendler 6 x 9, 208 pp, Quality PB, 978-1-58023-070-4 **$15.95**

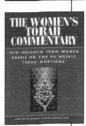

See Holidays for *The Women's Passover Companion: Women's Reflections on the Festival of Freedom* and *The Women's Seder Sourcebook: Rituals & Readings for Use at the Passover Seder.* Also see Bar/Bat Mitzvah for *The JGirl's Guide: The Young Jewish Woman's Handbook for Coming of Age.*

Travel

Israel—A Spiritual Travel Guide, 2nd Edition
A Companion for the Modern Jewish Pilgrim
By Rabbi Lawrence A. Hoffman 4¾ x 10, 256 pp, Quality PB, illus., 978-1-58023-261-6 **$18.99**
Also Available: **The Israel Mission Leader's Guide** 978-1-58023-085-8 **$4.95**

12-Step

Twelve Jewish Steps to Recovery: A Personal Guide to Turning from Alcoholism & Other Addictions—Drugs, Food, Gambling, Sex ...
By Rabbi Kerry M. Olitzky and Stuart A. Copans, MD; Preface by Abraham J. Twerski, MD
6 x 9, 144 pp, Quality PB, 978-1-879045-09-5 **$14.95**

About J

People of al   ge, educate,
and spiritua

Our princ   about who
the Jewish I   an be made
to hold. Wl   y audience,
our books s   oaden their
understandi

We bring   nought and
experience.   t in a voice
that you ca

Our book   nulate, and
inspire. We   re beautiful
and comme   ifference in
your life.

For your i   e have pro-
vided a list   nd useful.
They cover

Bar/B
Bible
Child
Cong
Curre   e
Ecol
Fictic   ,
Grief
Holi
Inspi
Kabb

, Publisher

Or pl   **shing**
Sunset Farm Offices, Route 4 • P.O. Box 237 • Woodstock, Vermont 05091
Tel: (802) 457-4000 • Fax: (802) 457-4004 • www.jewishlights.com
Credit card orders: **(800) 962-4544** (8:30AM–5:30PM ET Monday–Friday)
Generous discounts on quantity orders. SATISFACTION GUARANTEED. Prices subject to change.